Hedge Magic™

for Ars Magica,™ Fourth Edition

Aaron Link and John Snead

Table of Contents

Hedge Magic
CREDITS

Authors: Aaron Link and John Snead

Development, Editing, and Layout: Jeff Tidball

Editorial Assistance and Layout: John Nephew

Editorial Assistance: David Chart and Robbie Westmoreland

Cover Illustration: Charles Gillespie

Interior Illustrations: Eric Hotz, Jeff Menges, John Scotello, and Tonia Walden

Special Thanks: Bob Brynildson and Jerry Corrick

Playtesters: Tanja Bader, Chris Balow, Gordon Bowie-Reed, Bill Brickman, Rick Brooks, Chris Daianu, Michaël de Verteuil, Steve Drexler, Jim Dugger, Tamara Duran, Tom Erskine, John Garay, Alexander Gerber, Jochen Gutjahr, Ian Hargrove, Joan Hargrove, Karl Krumpholz, Scott Lien, Len McCain, Marc Messner, Stephen Mulholland, Jens Oesterle, Chris Page, Chris Roberts, Roderick Robertson, Robin Steeden, Sabine Völkel, and The Wanderer

About the Authors

John Snead is a 35 year old anthropologist living in Portland, Oregon. Discovering that a classic liberal arts education with degrees in mathematics, history, and anthropology makes one wholly unqualified for most ordinary forms of employment, John makes his (meager but happy) living as a freelance game writer and designer. John is also a long-time gamer, a practicing Wiccan priest, an amateur photographer, and an avid fan of SF and fantasy literature. John as written for **Ars Magica**, **Nephilim**, **Traveller**, and the upcoming SF RPG **Blue Planet**.

A Nebraska native, **Aaron Link** took a Masters Degree in the history and philosophy of science at the University of Wisconsin-Madison. Since then, he has dissected tigers in Wisconsin, reared scorpions and butterflies in San Diego, and guided school tours in south-central Los Angeles. His recent adventures include successfully completing sexual reassignment surgery last year. Other books by the artist formerly known as Sarah include *Shamans* and both editions of *Faeries* for **Ars Magica**, and the Alchemy sourcebook for **Nephilim**. Aaron Link currently works full-time as an artist and writer in Portland, Oregon.

Fans of **Ars Magica** discuss the game on an e-mail discussion list. To subscribe, send the command "subscribe ars-magica" (no quotes) in the body of an e-mail message to Majordomo@soda.Berkeley.EDU. To subscribe to a digest version of the list, send the command "subscribe ars-magica-digest" (no quotes) to the same address.

Project: Redcap archives and links to many of the fan-created **Ars Magica** pages on the World Wide Web. To get to Project: Redcap, point your browser at http://www.netforward.com/poboxes/?Redcap.

Errata for the first printing of the fourth edition of **Ars Magica** is available on request. Send a self-addressed, stamped envelope to PO Box 131233, Roseville, MN, 55113. Up-to-date errata is also posted on the Atlas Games World Wide Web site.

ATLAS GAMES

PO Box 131233
Roseville, MN 55113
E-mail: AtlasGames@aol.com
WWW: http://members.aol.com/atlasgames

ISBN 1-887801-58-8

Chapter 1
Introduction

Hedge Wizards in Mythic Europe

Mythic Europe is an innately magical place, populated with all manner of magical people and beasts—it is not simply historical Europe with the Order of Hermes grafted on. In addition to faeries, dragons, giants, werewolves, ghosts, and all manner of magical beasts, people can work magic. And not only those of the Order of Hermes. True, by the 13th century the Order has few competitors within the civilized portions of Mythic Europe. Gruagach practice in Scotland, Runemasters dominate the North, and Shamans populate the far corners of the known world, but none of these can claim to be as versatile, as well organized, or as numerous as the Order.

In this era Mythic Europe has a population of around 60 million people. Of these, a very small number, perhaps slightly more than 1000, have what Hermetic magi would call the Gift—that is, the ability to work Hermetic magic. Others also work magic, however. Whether these other magic-users lack a Gift or whether their Gifts are simply weaker than those of Hermetic magi is a matter open to much debate both within the Order and outside it.

In a sense, those who possess a single exceptional talent like as Second Sight, Hex, or Entrancement are working magic—and there are many such people in Mythic Europe. For our purposes, we must distinguish between people with minor talents and people who lack Hermetic abilities but nevertheless can perform sophisticated magic. An individual with an exceptional ability was likely born that way. Hedge wizards, on the other hand, possess special knowledge and training as well as inborn talent.

There are traditions of hedge wizardry with lineages as long as those of any Hermetic magi. In some cases, the only thing distinguishing hedge wizards from Hermetic magi is their level of raw power. Hermetic magi command a vast array of spells which can be loosed in seconds. For all groups of hedge wizards, all but the weakest of magics require preparations lasting from hours to months. Lively debate surrounds the question of whether hedge wizards have less inborn magical power than members of the Order (after all, most do not have what Hermetic magi would call the Gift), or whether the system of Bonisagus is simply a more effective way to work magic than any other yet found.

Those who are most unbiased note that there are three broad classes of people, as far as the ability to work magic is concerned. The first holds the vast majority of humanity; these are the unGifted, with no capacity to work magic. The second are those with the full, true Gift; these people have the capacity (if not the training) to work Hermetic magic. The third are those with only some ability to work magic; these people have a partial, damaged, or weak Gift. They do not have the capacity to learn Hermetic magic, but might still command some magical powers. The hedge wizards presented in this book come from the second and third classes.

Hedge wizards occupy a unique place within Mythic Europe. In many ways, hedge wizards are magi of the world. They may be found as advisors in the courts of kings, selling their wares in the great fairs, teaching at universities, and providing services to all sorts of people, from cunning courtiers to needy peasants. While many Hermetic magi are quite successful in escaping the need to participate in the economies of the world to acquire food and shelter, most hedge wizards are not so lucky. In fact, many hedge wizards maintain that the greater power of Hermetic magi comes from their greater success in removing themselves to isolation. Such thinkers often feel that the loss of their non-magical abilities is too high a price for greater magical power.

The vast majority of Hermetic magi see hedge wizardry as wholly beneath their notice. For example, if a hedge wizard were to become court wizard to a powerful king, most magi of the Order would simply smile smugly at his pretension. Of course, the vast majority of magi of the Order know next to nothing about the vast array of minor magics which abound in Mythic Europe, simply because they have never bothered to look closely.

In this book, we describe four traditions of hedge wizardry. These are not the only traditions in Mythic Europe, simply four that are common. Furthermore, they are four that offer a good deal of variety, spanning many of the concepts that might lead a player to want to try playing a hedge wizard.

The cunning-folk live close to the land and know many of its secrets. While they work magic, they often know much of faerie things—sometimes cunning-folk are considered touched by faeries. Scholars and magi usually underestimate the cunning-folk, but their charms and potions can contain great power. Furthermore, they often have a freedom to move in all levels of society, an ability which is almost unique in Mythic Europe. At the same time, they can inspire as much fear, awe, or respect in most ordinary people as a Hermetic magus can.

The natural magicians represent the newest of the four traditions. Natural magicians have learned some of the magical secrets found in works from the classical era. As such, their magic is in many ways similar to that practiced by Hermetic magi. Natural magicians are found throughout the cities and universities of Europe, and are sometimes seen in the courts of kings.

Spirit masters follow a very old tradition. They bargain for the services of spirits of all kinds, sometimes fairly, sometimes using trickery. Because some spirits are malevolent, and because their charismatic summonings sometimes attract Infernal powers, spirit masters are often reputed to deal with Hell. A few do deal with demons, but they are not generally diabolists. Instead, they seek to trick demons into performing their bidding. The vast majority of spirit masters maintain that they only deal with unaffiliated spirits, such as elementals and ghosts.

The ascetics are the most mysterious of these four traditions. As a result of meditation and austerity, ascetics can take their bodies and minds beyond the mundane limits of the world. Ascetics claim they learn to perceive the truth behind the coarse veil of the mortal world. Many also claim these perceptions bring them closer to God. Some see ascetics as heretics, others as saviors. While most ascetics are content to retire quietly from the world, a few promote justice, compassion, or the unimportance of earthly powers, much to the displeasure of many lords and bishops.

Herbalists and alchemists can also be considered hedge wizards. Both the herbalist and alchemist must be trained, and both have a greater versatility than those who possess but one inborn talent. Herbalists are found in may villages, and alchemists in many cities. In fact, in the largest cities, alchemists have even started their own guilds where standards of training and learning are even higher. Still, herbalists, and alchemists are the lowest level of hedge wizards.

Minor Magics in Christendom

by Rebecca of House Mercere, chief librarian of Harco

There is magic all around us. We of the Order fail to notice much of it. That which we notice we usually dismiss as trickery.

In the early days of the Order such attitudes were reasonable. We were concerned only with those possessing the Gift. Magi with the Gift were either members of the Order, thereby our comrades, or were persuaded to join. Those who declined were destroyed. Those without the Gift were beneath our notice.

Those days are gone. The rogue magi who used to populate Christendom now linger only in legends and tales. With few exceptions, the only Gift-possessing magi within the bounds of Christendom are members of our Order.

Some now seek to learn from those magi who live beyond the borders of Christendom, such as the Council of Sulieman which holds sway in the Levant and in Moorish Spain. However, some small instruction can also be taken by looking more closely at the magics and magi which still exist within the bounds of Christendom.

We dismiss those without the Gift as hedge wizards, and rightly so. Such folk lack the talent and learning to take their place within the Order. Moreover, their spells and other magic are of little use to us. However, there are reasons for us to briefly study hedge magic and its practitioners. There are many more alchemists, witches, charm-makers and natural philosophers than there are members of our Order. These limited wizards live in villages and in cities. They make their living providing services to mundanes. In Venice and in Paris the alchemists have their own guilds.

We live in our covenants, isolated from those who live around us. Most folk who live in Christendom know nothing but fanciful legends about the members of our Order. However, most have seen the witch who lives in their village, or the natural philosopher who teaches in their city. Undoubtedly, most are ignorant even of the difference between hedge wizards and Hermetic magi. Hedge wizards represent the sum and total of what most mundanes know of magic. Hedge wizards are useful for what they can teach about how mundanes will react to us. If nothing else, it is undeniable that they move more freely within mortal society than most of us do. At some time, this knowledge may be useful to us.

Furthermore, while the magic of hedge wizardry is limited, it may serve as a guide to the various and sundry shapes magic takes in the world. All know that the methods of Bonisagus are but one way of codifying magic. Perhaps by looking at the magics hedge wizards perform we will learn how to expand on our own magics.

In this spirit I present three reports which have been given to me on hedge magics within Christendom.

From Superbus of Bonisagus

I am asked about magic in Christendom. There is magic throughout Christendom, and its existence should serve as a lesson to us.

Mundanes cannot see spirits or feel the power which makes a pool whose water abounds in vis different from a pool of ordinary water. However, in most villages and hamlets there will be someone who has what they will call "The Sight," or some similar talent.

However, these folk are merely touched by magic, they have a small gift which they can often neither rely on nor explain. Their presence is no marker of ability or wisdom. People who possess magic but are bereft of training are the most common, but also the most limited of those who can work magics.

Hedge wizards, in their own primitive way, undergo training. Similarly, one who plays the lute so as to make stones weep works something like magic, which requires both gift and skill. A mundane performer could never make a rock weep, but an unskilled performer would fail to make anyone weep, except perhaps at how badly he mangles a favored song. People who possess magic and also training are rare, but they are capable of much greater use of what gift they possess.

As with all things there is variation. Both the quality of magic, and the quality of training are immensely greater in a magus of the Order than in even the most skilled village witch.

The existence of hedge witches should serve as a warning to all members of the Order. Without great care and the wondrous system of Bonisagus we could be little better than they. A pure Gift and our founder's teachings are necessary to produce a magus fit to join the Order. A pure Gift and imperfect training, or training in the system of our founder and a damaged Gift produces hedge magi and fools.

Hedge magi can are best seen as a lesson, the lesson being that what is most pure is also most rare.

From Anthonius of Jerbiton

When I needed supplies recently, I had occasion to journey to the market at Paris. I was greatly surprised to find several merchants selling a small quantity of stones and animal parts which contained vis.

I was concerned that these were being sold to some other covenant, which had perhaps settled in the area without our knowledge. When I asked the merchants who sold these wares, they told me instead to seek a few scholars who had newly arrived into town.

I had heard of the new college, but had been lead to expect priceless books and unruly students rather than scholars buying raw vis in the market-place. I spoke with several of the university scholars and have learned something quite amazing. It appears that mundane scholars and students are trying to learn the art of Hermetic magic.

They call what they do natural magic. In many ways it owes more to the tawdry magics of alchemists with their vile-smelling shops. However, these natural magicians have higher aspirations than making potions which aid healing or keep vain ladies looking young. Natural magicians study the classics as we do, they share information with each other, and they seek to shape magic to the tasks at hand.

It is quite sad that these well-intentioned, and often brilliant individuals lack the true Gift. They must work their magic through the use of elaborate rituals—with incense and stones, colored cloth, and astrological symbols.

It is quite sad to see them struggle with their props to perform magics any member of the Order could perform in seconds with no need for externals. However, these natural magicians are fine scholars, and some have books our Order lacks.

Natural magicians do not belong in the Order. Still, some may be persuaded to become most able lab assistants, while others may prove useful partners in scholarship. Those I have met lack the Gift. In spite of this lack, these scholars work magic like unto ours. While they are much less able than we, that they succeed at all may be worthy of more study. Finally, while they are not our equals, they do not fear us, and conversation with them can be both pleasing and informative.

From the Journal of Passer of Mercere

In my travels I have seen many strange things, however, there are three which stick forever in my memory. The first of these was frightening, the second wonderful and good, and the third strange beyond my knowledge.

Many years ago, I was riding through the eastern part of the Black Forest. Late one evening, I came to a small village. The inhabitants were rude foresters who welcomed me with the hospitality common to such folk. I was put up in the house of the couple who seemed to lead this village. After an uncommonly fine roast for dinner, we talked of the world beyond this forest, and I provided news of the surrounding area as well as several stories and songs unfamiliar to ones as isolated as they. Then I retired for the night.

Later, I awoke to the sounds of people moving around me. I grasped my knife and lay still lest this trouble bode ill for me. After a bit, the couple and their daughter left, and I could hear the sounds of more people outside. When I looked cautiously out into the moonlit night, I saw the entire population of the village, perhaps a dozen folk and a few children, walking towards a nearby hill. I could hear them talking softly as they walked.

I followed cautiously and at some distance. When they were perhaps half-way to the hill I witnessed a most terrifying spectacle. All the villagers, even the children, shed their clothes and took the shapes of wolves.

When they approached the hill, there was a woman standing there. She wore the garb of a wealthy traveler and appeared quite unsurprised at the appearance of the villager-wolves. She talked to them, addressing them as if they were people she was bargaining with in market. I could not hear what was being said and decided that it might be unsafe to remain. I returned to the village, got on my horse, and rode until after dawn.

In the first village I found outside of the forest I asked about what I had seen. No one knew of the woman, but several people told stories of the village of werewolves in the forest. Since then I have heard other stories of mysterious wizards who deal with dark creatures.

Several years later I was traveling through the south of France when I came upon a dark fen reputed to be a faerie area. I was rather apprehensive at entering this forest, since my last encounter with the fair folk had left me with a pair of asses ears. Pulling my cap low on my head, I journeyed quickly to the forest.

I encountered nothing untoward until I had almost reached the other side. I heard and then saw a middle-aged man dressed as a peasant defending himself against four gray and gnarled creatures who were clawing and biting at him. He wielded his staff well, but they outnumbered him. I drew my sword and joined the fray. In a short while we had dispatched the fell creatures.

In the course of the battle I had received a deep slash on my leg. The man, whose name was Gerard, helped me back to his solitary hut which was a short walk from the fen. Inside, the profusion of herbs, stones, and mysterious bundles made his profession quite plain.

I had met herbalists in the past, but none such as Gerard. Not only did he tend to my wound so that it healed in but a few days, he also was able to restore my ears to their normal state by applying a poultice.

As I had no messages at the time, and had been traveling in search of a cure for my recent affliction, I decided to stay with Gerard for some time. He seemed to greatly enjoy the company since the people in the nearby villages were a stolid lot and little inclined to conversation or pleasantries when they were seeking his aid.

Gerard spoke to me of herbs and beasts and of living close to the land, while I told him the many tales of my travels. Unlike some like him I had met before, Gerard was quite educated and well spoken in his own quiet way. He spoke often of his teacher and how he had worked for her for many years before she deemed him ready to work on his own. At the end of my stay, Gerard made two charms for use against malefic faeries. One he kept, and the other he gave to me, asking no price but that I come visit again when I was next in the south of France.

The last of these three encounters took place last year. I was journeying from Spain to France when a mountain bandit who styled himself lord of the region sent his men out to take me prisoner. I'm as brave as any, but when faced with a dozen men, on good horses, armed and armored with steel, there was no choice but surrender. I was taken to the ruined pile of stones this lord called his keep, and imprisoned in a deep cell. This cur knew of Redcaps and was certain that he could extract a goodly ransom from the Order.

The next day the guards brought in another traveler. This one was a young man in simple dress who they had beaten severely. I tended to his wounds, which turned out not to be serious. He told me that the folk of the nearby village had sent him to bargain with these thugs to accept a portion of the villagers' harvest in return for halting their raids and violence.

The bandits' response was to beat the man and inform him that they could and would take any-thing they wanted. He told me they planned to cut off his hands and send him back to the village with this message. I saw no way to escape, and feared that there was nothing I could do to help him avoid this grim fate. He appeared uncon-cerned, and told me that the trials of the world could not touch those who could see beyond it.

From talking to him, it was clear that the vil-lagers had sent him because he was a holy man, and also far too clear that this fact would not save him from the bandits. Samuel, for that was his name, asked me to pray with him, which I did, though his prayers were not those I knew. Then, after a time, when the guards were asleep, he asked me if the Order would free me if they knew where I was, and if there were those in it who could do so. I told him that the magi of Duresca, from whence I had just come, were but a day's hard ride away, and that they could rescue us both with ease if they but knew my plight.

He then asked me if I had anything from Duresca. I showed him my pouch of messages. Samuel asked if he could take the pouch for a bit, saying that with it he would be able to free the both of us. Not knowing if this were hope or delusion, I agreed. Samuel then took my message pouch, and went to the far side of the room. He drew symbols in the dirt on the floor and sat amidst them. For the next long while he appeared lost in deep and fervent prayer. I assumed he was praying for a miracle, for the symbols were like none I had seen in any type of magic.

After a time he rose, and I could feel the change in him. It was like light came from his body. Samuel then wished me well, took up my pouch and promised that aid would come to me soon. Then he vanished, like he had never been here at all. Others would say what happened was a miracle, but I could feel that it was some kind of magic.

In the morning the bandits came for me, and seeing that Samuel was gone grew most alarmed. Their leader asked me how he had escaped. I replied that he had vanished while I was asleep. The other bandits counseled beating me until I revealed the truth, but their leader feared that doing so might spoil the ransom.

I was promised that I would not eat until I revealed where he had gone and then taken back to the cell. Late that night the rocks fell away from the side of the cell and Veritas of Duresca stood there surrounded by his grogs. Veritas and Tacitus then brought the keep down on the heads of the bandits inside.

As we rode away I asked how I came to be rescued. Veritas told me that a slender young man had appeared late the night before and handed the guard a message pouch which he said was to be given to the Magi. The man then left before the guard returned. The message pouch was mine and contained the note Samuel had asked me to write describing our location and my plight. When Veritas and the others used their magics to try to locate Samuel, they failed entirely.

All I can say is that whatever Samuel did to escape the cell was magic of some unknown type. A Criamon I once talked to said that there were some for whom faith was magical, but that is all I know.

Chapter 2
The Mystery of Michael Scot

The Hedge Wizards' Story

Sibylle the Ascetic's Story

When I first saw Michael Scot three months ago he worried me. He is fair, and well-spoken, but he had an air of pride about himself that made me doubt him. The stories you told me of the displays he put on in the contest to become Frederick's personal wizard may have been most wondrous. Still, all of his flash and his fair speech seemed to mask something darker. I looked closely at him and could see no hint of corruption, but I was not satisfied.

After the feast where he was formally chosen by Frederick, I meditated and looked deep within myself to see if my worries were real or merely an old woman's foolishness. My light within was answered by the light without, and I knew that Michael Scot sought to harm Frederick.

For all your kindness, Elaine, I know well how everyone at court sees me. Crazy Sibylle, with her uncombed hair. They are all either too blind or too fearful to see truth when it is presented to them. Frederick asked my advice once, but only

Historical Note

Several of the characters in this story are based on historical figures.

Sibylle actually was the second wife of Roger II of Sicily, born in 1126. She married Roger II in 1149, a few years before his death. All other information about her in this narrative is fiction and speculation.

Albertus is Albertus Magnus (1193-1280), a magician and philosopher. He wrote many books including a book on astronomy and astrology entitled *The Mirror of Astronomy* and a book on alchemy called *On Alchemy*. It is also said that he was the author of a well-known book on natural magic called *The Book of Secrets*. Legends say he created a bronze head which could speak like a person. Albertus became the Bishop of Ratisbon and the teacher of St. Thomas Aquinas during his lifetime. Albert himself was canonized in 1932.

Michael Scot (1175-1234) is a complex figure about whom there are many legends and few facts. Born in Scotland, he traveled widely. He studied at Oxford, Paris, Bologna, and most of the other universities of Europe, becoming a mathematician, astrologer, alchemist, physician, and scholar. He translated the first European editions of Aristotle and Avicenna as well as writing *Liber Introductorius*, a textbook on natural magic and necromancy. Michael Scot was reputed to summon faeries, ghosts, and demons. He became Frederick II's court wizard around 1220.

One story about Michael Scot says he stole the secret of calculating the date of Easter from the Pope. In spite of his reputation as a magician, he was once offered the bishopric of Cashel, in Ireland, by Pope Honorius III, who was also allegedly a magician.

when he had no where else to turn. To announce, without proof, that his wonderful new wizard plotted against him would serve no purpose. Still, blind as he is, Frederick is wise for a king, and I would not have his work rebuilding Sicily undone.

I told no one, not even you, of my thoughts. Instead I sought further advice from the light. After much reflection I decided to seek those who knew Michael Scot and ask them of his intentions.

He studied magic at Padua, so to Padua I decided to go. I am sorry I could not tell you more of my journey before I left, but at least I can remedy this now. My journey beyond this tawdry shell into the pure realm and back again was as glorious as always.

Padua is much as I remember it. The innkeeper who runs the Dove remembered me after all these years. She was so young when I saw her last—now her hair has all gone gray. She let me stay at the inn and provided me with meals.

I did not have to look far in Padua to find someone who remembered Michael Scot. I met a man named Rogerius, also from Scotland, who had known Michael Scot in Padua. He seemed a wise man, for someone who does not seek the truth within. Rogerius was overjoyed to hear of Michael Scot's appointment as Frederick's wizard. He answered many questions about Michael Scot, but provided me with nothing useful. I refrained from asking him about my suspicions; perhaps this was foolish.

I did learn that Michael Scot had upset many of the holy men in Padua, but that his silver tongue had saved him. Perhaps there is something to this, but I too have been on the wrong side of foolish and narrow-minded Clerics.

I talked to many others in Padua, and read some writings of Michael Scot's that Rogerius had kept, but learned nothing more. It seems Michael Scot has had other teachers and associates in other lands. Perhaps this whole journey has been in vain. I would have returned, but I noticed something most odd—I was being followed. A young man who carries himself like a nobleman has been following me. He has made no move to approach me, and clearly thinks me unaware of his attentions.

This morning I saw another man with him. I grew concerned and sought answers from the light as to why these men were following me. My fears were confirmed. I found that they follow me because I am interested in Michael Scot.

I fear I may have stumbled into a rather deep plot. I will close this letter with my seal, and write upon it that you should not open it unless a season passes without my return. After I send this letter, I will confront these men.

Agnes the Cunning-woman's Story

I was his first teacher, for good or ill only God himself knows, but it was I that first set his foot upon the path. I'll set it down in writing now for anyone to see.

He was but a boy then, come to the cunning-woman for learning with his eyes all burning bright. I'd seen those eyes in the head of Richard the Mad who killed his kinsmen for their power, and Elsie NicEwin who lost first her mind and then her soul. When Michael Scot first came to me I thought, "That boy will do what he will do, and neither God nor the Devil will stop him. If he's for knowing and for power, its best he be getting it right."

So I raised him and I taught him before the swordsmen could take him with their blood-thirst or the faeries could bear him away. If I live to see the Highlands worn low I may never have a quicker student. I taught him the gifts of land and water, and reading and writing, and manners pleasing to men and women and the good folk alike. Mark that I taught him charms before banes, and ten of the one for each of the other. And when I could teach him no more I knew he was no ordinary man. So I sent him far across the sea, into the keeping of friends at Padua.

For twenty years I've heard nothing of him but his name, his fame, and his fortune. Last night he came to me, still a proud boy, weeping like his heart would break.

"Agnes, come and see me, for I've opened up a book I cannot put away," he said to me. He held his hands out, and when I came to take them I was

in my own room and he a great man, a thousand miles over the sea.

God doesn't have to send me warning twice. I prepared the brew in a place I know, and drank it with those who abide there, and told them all the trouble. When I departed I left cakes and salt, but before I left they gave me counsel.

I saw a great court, far across the sea, and a hundred gentlemen and ladies fair, all dressed in finery. They drank from cups of silver and gold and watched strange entertainments: flying hawks and dancing Saracens. First among them was a man dressed as a king. At his right hand was Michael Scot, wearing silk worked thick with gold in letters, some in Latin, some in a tongue I think was Saracen. This king liked him well. Behind the king there stood a woman in a plain white dress. Her face I will not forget. Her hair was wild, her bearing like a noble born, not shamed before the others' finery. For all the world she was like a woman of the fay. Behind my Michael Scot someone was standing, too. It was a darkness standing like a man, more braggart than the King of England. I didn't have to see its face to know its black heart. It had its arms around his shadow like a lover, its hand upon his shoulder, and when it raised its hand proud Michael Scot did dance just like a puppet on a string. No more than that would I see. I left my thanks and went home to wrap up bread and cheese and fill a wineskin. Whatever he's done, he was my student. Whatever has hold of him, he came to me for help, and I'll not refuse him.

I set out for Padua. I thought that my friends there might know of Michael Scot's whereabouts. Or if not, they would at least be able to tell me where to start.

The journey to Padua was a long, hard one, and I had not traveled so far in my body for many years. Though God gives the means for me to make the travel easier for all who go with me, times come when I envy the magi their wonders. Ah well, if the back of a donkey was good enough for Our Lord, and the ships of the sea wonder enough for the good folk, then they're good enough for me.

In Padua I found Roger Glendower, though they call him Rogerius here. He's a teacher, and the years have made him far more a scholar of Padua than the Scots monk I first knew. It is a good friendship that cares not for years and places, and he greeted me with as much joy as I hailed him.

"Agnes ," said he, "What wind has blown you out of the wilderness and into the center of civilization?"

"Ill wind enough, I fear," said I.

"What, have you lost your Latin entirely, and must come to us for a refresher?"

"I have enough yet to riddle you blind in your scholar's tongue, old friend, and my wilderness is civilized enough to give you a place by the fire and a drink before we must talk of harder things."

"Of course," said he, "come in and rest. The table is laid for supper when you wish, and you are welcome to stay."

We drank wine and water instead of mead, and our fire was a garden full of flowers such as they paint in pictures of Paradise, but it was old times again between us, late into the night. It was a picture I hated to spoil. Finally, before the dawn Roger's curiosity would not be stilled, and again he asked,

"What brings you so many leagues from home? You seem too serious in mind for pilgrimage."

"You've a quick eye for faces still, Roger Glendower. 'Tis not pilgrimage for my soul, but for our friend Michael Scot. You know where he may be found?"

"Who here does not, Agnes? He's scored a signal triumph. He's been named court wizard to King Frederick of Sicily this spring. He's there now, pulling pigs out of pouches, hares from hats, and armies from the nail of his little finger for the amusement of the court."

"And what else, Roger? Have you heard aught of him that the criers wouldn't tell?"

His broad face furrowed up. "What is this about Michael Scot? Agnes, you're not the first to ask me of him in the past few weeks. What's he done? Why haven't I heard?"

"Someone else has asked after him? Tell me quickly, who and when."

"The strangest woman I've ever met came here a few weeks ago, asking about the wizard Michael Scot and his teachers. I told her that I had known him here, and I remembered him very well indeed."

"What did you tell her?"

"How he'd nearly had us all driven out of the city and excommunicated, and then wooed us back to favor so well that the archbishop nearly strewed orchids in our path. Old stories. She seemed looking for some black mark against his name, but hardly satisfied with what I told her. I'm not sure she knew what she was looking for."

"Tell me more of her."

"Not till you tell me what all this is about. God knows that you and I both had joy and grief enough from him."

So I told him all, of the dream and the vision. And when I told him his face went pale.

"God's blood, Agnes. The faerie woman—it was her came to me asking of Michael Scot!"

"She wasn't one of the good people, Roger. They would have told me if she was. I'm a stranger to the custom of this country. Do you know what else she could be? Perhaps a nun?"

"Perhaps a heretic. Some of them keep strange customs. But she spoke nothing to me of God or of the sinfulness of priests and scholars in the costume of the Church. They always sing that song like nightingales, night and day alike."

"How would I find out more of her?"

"I know where she's staying. She asked if I would speak to anyone else who knew him, and send word if I found anything out. I can give you the address and send a link-boy to guide your way. Be careful, for I know no more of this than you've told me."

"God bless you for a good friend, Roger Glendower."

I took the address and the link-boy and I went.

Nicolai the Spirit Master's Story

I had need of a good horse. The Germans were playing at knights again, going on Crusades against log houses full of farmers and their goats. It makes me tired. The screaming keeps a poor merchant awake. So I drew the circle in mare's piss and waited, and before long seven horses came by, mares and stallions.

They were all good horses. I had not seen so many in one place before. I saw their heads turn, one by one, to me and my circle, but neither the mare's piss nor my call could move them—someone else was calling. They went on as though drawn together by one rope, heading South. I tried the circle three days later and saw two more good horses heading South along the same path. None but they and I could see it, but it was there all the same.

So I had to handle the Germans without a good horse. It made me tired.

I had need of a magus. I had called one before, a fire-man from the Order of Hermes. They do not love to be called to circle if they learn they have been called, for their vanity is measureless. But this one was renowned as an advisor to kings and warriors. He knew the powers of the Hermetics, and had fought Christian knights and armies enough to know the strength and weakness both of their arms and their faith. It is useful knowledge, and hard to find. Besides, their vanity keeps them from telling others that they have been called. It is better to know more of one's neighbors than they know of you, so their contempt serves me well.

I drew the circle with a stick of charcoal I had. It was the kind of thing that makes their eyes go crazy like a hungry dog and their hands go reaching. I drew the circle thick and kept fires burning at the cardinal points, fed them an incense I knew he would like. Sooner or later they always come, whether they will bargain or not. It's like baiting with a carcass for flies.

I waited for a week.

Then I grew restless, and added other inducements. He sent a message. The fires of my circle spoke to me. They said,

"I regret that I am unable to attend your conference. Should another be held at some time in the future, I would come. The topics are very interesting to me and the promised accommodations sound extremely attractive. Unfortunately, I am committed to a previous engagement, a horsemen's conference with Michael Scot that will demand my complete attention in Italy for some time."

I saw the bond upon my magus was the same bond that had drawn so many good horses from my country. So I grew curious and sent a messenger to Italy. The answer came back that Michael Scot is the court wizard of the king of Sicily. The king of Sicily is a falconer, but not much of a horseman. My messenger could find no trace of a horsemen's conference. A curious conference of horsemen that takes place without the knowledge of the king, and takes the attention of magi for some time.

There is a rumor that the price of furs in Sicily is now extremely high. I believe I shall take my humble wares and go. Perhaps the king will buy, or perhaps this Michael Scot and I will have some commerce concerning the price of things that have been taken from me.

Albertus the Natural Magician's Story

I had come to Padua on the business of the Church, but when it was concluded I found I had sufficient time to learn something of the city. In speaking with some other learned men in the city, I met a man named Rogerius. We fell to talking, and he mentioned a document he had that was written by a man he knew, Michael Scot, who had recently been named court wizard of Frederick II. What he said interested me, and I asked to read it. Rogerius agreed.

In it, Michael Scot claims the authority of no ancient source, and comments on no sacred writing. The work explains, barefaced, that it is original, deserving of consideration entirely on its own merits, for neither ancient philosophers nor the fathers of the Church adequately considered the subject. Its subject is the division of invisible powers according to their natures. It claims that too much has been made of the distinction among the different sorts of mortal men and women who use invisible powers. According to the document, magi, natural magicians, those who call upon the holy power of God, the users of Infernal powers offered to mortals as temptations, the sorcerers known among pagans and Saracens, and all others who use invisible powers may be considered as one kind. Michael Scot avoids direct blasphemy by recognizing that the source of these powers may be very different, and lead to very different spiritual consequences. Yet he maintains that not enough attention has been paid to the similarity of these powers in their practical effects. The rest of the document is a closely-reasoned analysis of the uses of invisible powers in the world.

The analysis is brilliant. It could serve as a plan for someone wishing to rise in station, become a famous scholar, conquer a country, or gain great wealth. The plan is practical but general, and could serve for any sort of application of its principles. The first section is an extraordinary exercise in rhetoric, designed to defend the moral implications of this sort of thinking. It is so well done that not even a Dominican superior could find heresy in it. Yet the thought of what could become of us if this document became popular keeps me awake at night. It seems clear to me that the Order of Hermes, using it, could certainly establish an empire. However, the theory requires accepting that all invisible powers are equal in their practical effects, and experience shows how reluctant the Order is to admit to equals. A less pious writer than I could say the same thing of Mother Church. Perhaps this is why it is hidden away with Rogerius in Padua, rather than at the right hand of kings or burned long ago.

I began to inquire further of this Michael Scot. He seems to have made a vivid impression on those who remain in Padua. Though he trained in natural magic here, he seems to have begun as a peasant magician in Scotland. One cannot help but wonder if he is following his own plan. This thought also kept me awake at night.

The first curious thing happened when I went back to talk to Rogerius, to ask if he had any of Michael Scot's other writing preserved. He told me that some of it was not available at the moment, as it was being read by another. I went to find the reader, who he said had gone to a place nearby, and discovered an unkempt old woman in a white shift, reading the Latin documents with great attention. Her face was not the face of the old woman she was. The look she gave me, a man of learning and high birth, for disturbing her should have come from a lady with a queen's garments. I decided to be discreet, and waited for the documents to be returned.

In a spirit of experiment, I began to inquire in the pharmacies and book stalls of Padua as I went about my own exploration of the city. Many of the older shopkeepers remember Michael Scot quite clearly. He seems to be the sort of man who made a strong impression. Records and memory both agree that he practiced as a natural magician here, and bought large quantities of books and materials. Though only a student, his reputation was great, and he practiced for more profit than many of his teachers. His tastes were eclectic. I have found record of him among the merchants who sell Saracen goods, as well as among the Jews. I freely admit that my own needs did not bring me to such people. At this point, I was pursuing the inquiry like a hound on a scent.

When I had exhausted the possibilities of research, I was moved to direct experience. It seemed to me that we could speak, as one natural magician to another. Therefore, I prepared materials and attempted to contact him from Padua. To my surprise, I discovered that Michael Scot is not only protected by invisible powers, but that he is blocked from all contact. I made several experiments and was unable to find any way to reach him.

At this point, I was ready to conclude my research upon Michael Scot. Though I was curious, I have discovered that court wizards make tiresome pretense to greatness. I had no wish to travel to Sicily to be kept waiting for weeks in order to improve the standing of a man who must be seen by some as an upstart barbarian. However, the appearance of the monster changed my plans.

It came through the wall of my room, at the common inn where I was staying. The creature was an airy spirit with the face of a lion and the body of a leper, and it had come to speak with me.

"Leave off your harrying," it said. "The scent you follow will bring you nothing but grief."

"I will follow what scent I please with the reason God gave me," I said, for I did not like its tone of threat, "and I fear nothing that comes from truth."

"Then you will find your prey is too large for you. I do not warn a third time."

"Good. Be gone to the place you came from. I meant no harm to Michael Scot, but you are mistaken to think you can order me off like a dog."

It became clear at this point that I had misunderstood the creature. It did not leave, but came at me like a dog of war. Though I defended myself well, it is possible that the spirit had made an accurate estimate of the situation. I was deprived of the opportunity to find out by the man who battered down my door and roared at the spirit in a voice of thunder, words that I did not understand. The spirit removed itself from my body, and spoke with the man for a few moments in this foreign tongue. Then it was gone again, and the stranger was warding off the landlord. My offer to pay for the door sent him away, and the stranger and I sat down to talk.

He was a curious man, with the dress of a noble, the manners of an Easterner, and the broad, flat face of a barbarian. A kingfisher sat upon his shoulder like a trained crow, and seemed little disturbed by the trouble. The man spoke Latin with no accent at all.

"You drew no circle. You should draw a circle in your room each night."

"But I do not summon spirits."

"Of course. If you had been stupid enough to bring leprosy to yourself without protection, I would have let it have you. But if your enemies can send you spirits, you should learn to draw a circle."

"I had no idea that I had enemies who would send me hostile spirits. Who are you? What did you do with it? Is it coming back?"

The stranger smiled. "You may call me Nicolai," he said, "and it is not coming back. I gave it to a local monk. It will be satisfied by now."

It struck me suddenly that if he had such power over the spirit, he must have summoned it, but I could not see why he would have it attack me and then call it off. If he wished to prove himself my friend, he would surely have chosen a story that showed him a better man than this one did. I thought quickly and then spoke.

"I no longer feel safe here without knowing how to send such a spirit away. What is your price for instructing me in the method you used?"

"My price," said the man, "is low, since the instruction is of questionable worth. Tell me how you believe you gained the spirit's attention, and I will tell you how I sent it away."

"Agreed," said I.

Nicolai explained that the monk had come to him, offering gold in exchange for the power to force women to his will. The monk would not be discouraged, and Nicolai finally gave his price as a debt from the monk, to be collected whenever and in whatever fashion pleased Nicolai. To his surprise, the monk agreed, and they concluded a pact. Nicolai had simply told the spirit he knew of less dangerous prey, and suggested he was willing to offer up his boon for the spirit's satisfaction. Later, I was able to discover that the monk Nicolai had described lived nearby, and had a reputation both as a lecher and an impious man.

In my turn I told the story of my researches concerning Michael Scot. When I mentioned the name, his curious eyes took fire.

"The mystery is explained," said he, "for Michael Scot is a master of spirits, and I believe he prepares some business he wishes kept secret."

"But Michael Scot is a natural magician. I have met with those who knew him."

"Then he must be both, for I have seen the spirits brought to meet him, across land and river, from a great distance."

"It is a marvel I have never before heard of, that one man should be both. I would speak with this Michael Scot."

Nicolai smiled a little, then. "I also have business with him."

We fell to talking then, and shared our findings. Though he was without mercy, I found Nicolai had a quick mind, wide learning, and a strong sense of justice. As we spoke, I came to trust his judgment, and we found ourselves sharing our plans as well. Nicolai believed Michael Scot was on the edge of some great work of magic. Knowing his theories of power, I had to believe his plans were for some material gain.

Though it seemed necessary to take some action, we were at a loss for what to do. Then I thought of the strange woman reading Michael Scot's other works.

"Someone besides ourselves is interested in Michael Scot. I saw a woman of some will asking about him, though I do not know if she is his friend or foe."

"Then we can follow her until we know more."

"I can find her, Nicolai, but it seems dishonorable to follow a lone woman in a foreign city."

"I am sure," said he, "that your conduct with the leprosy was most honorable. If she is one of Michael Scot's servants, I am sure she will appreciate your delicacy."

I thought for a moment. "It is possible that you have a valid point."

The next morning, I determined the location of the woman, and we set out together.

We followed her through the day, but I quickly began to feel a fool. She went about in the most innocent fashion. Wherever she walked, children and foreigners would stop to speak with her, and the sick asked her to touch them, as if she were a sacred relic. She answered all requests with the same distant smile. When she entered a cathedral I finally refused to harry her further.

We agreed to return to her home and wait to see what she did when she arrived. Just before dark she arrived with a market basket. Nicolai crept close to the window, then returned.

"What is she doing?"

"She is setting a table for supper, for three people. She is doing it herself, and I can see no sign of servants."

"That is strange, and more strange if she expects visitors. Do your spirits eat?"

"She is not of my kind...."

At this moment, the door opened, and the woman we had followed called out: "The table is set, gentlemen. Please come in for supper. I am sure we have much to talk about."

She gave us nothing but bread and cheese, served on the fine white plates of a wealthy house. Nicolai did not seem to mind, and I remembered early lessons and said nothing. Later, I learned that the bread and cheese had likely been gifts from the market people, and the fine house was not her own. Sibylle de Bourgogne, the widow of a king, moved through the world upon the power of charity, and lived by gifts of those who were grateful for the healings, blessing, and advice she had given them. She spoke to us meekly, but I saw the fierce intelligence behind her eyes. One does not survive long dressed as a beggar at court without it.

She told us her story of Michael Scot. Her tale was honest and complete, so that it seemed she held nothing from us. For that reason, and because we did not know how else to proceed, I told her my own. Since my story involved Nicolai, he too told what he knew, though he is a secretive man. By the time we finished speaking, the darkness lay deep over Padua. We sat before the light of a single candle, within the chalk circle Nicolai had drawn upon the floor, attempting to put together the puzzle of Michael Scot's plans.

"We can make no effective plan of action until we know not only his methods but also his goals," said I. "I have tried to contact him, as a fellow scholar and a brother practitioner, but he has isolated himself from all magical inquiry."

"Then we must go to Sicily," said Nicolai. "We do nothing sitting here." He stared impatiently out the window.

"I fear Michael Scot has little sympathy for a woman whose costume is so much plainer than his wizard's robes. He has no wish to see me. The light tells me to be wary of him, yet the others at court do not see this as I do. We cannot count on many allies."

"I found it dangerous to press him, especially if we gain nothing of practical value by doing so. It seems unlikely he will trust any of us," said I.

"There is a torch-bearer coming down the street." Nicolai's voice was low and sharp. "There is someone with him. I think they are coming here."

He drew a long dagger from his robe and held it flat beneath the table. Sibylle stared at nothing for a long moment, then spoke softly.

"I do not think she means us harm."

There was a knock at the door. Sibylle rose and opened it. From the hall I heard an old woman's voice, speaking Latin with a strong island accent.

"My name is Agnes, and I've come a long way to see you. I'm Michael Scot's teacher, and I'd know what you wish of me." Sibylle brought her into the room. Agnes frowned at the cold hearth and the single candle. She turned and left the room, returning with the link-boy's spare torch.

"I've not much to my name," said she, "but I can at least bring you a fire to warm your hands by, and a bit of light in all the darkness. You may be a great lady, and gentlemen all, but I'll ask you to humor an old woman none the less for it, and tell me what you would have of Michael Scot."

Sibylle showed her to a seat, and I introduced us all. It was Sibylle who first answered the question.

"I come from Sicily, where Michael Scot dwells as wizard to the court. His ways were round-about and I was uncertain of him, for purity has nothing to hide." I saw Nicolai smile faintly into his beard as she spoke. "The light told me to be wary of him, for he was a danger to the king. When I asked the light for help I was told to seek his teacher. It seems you have been sent to aid us."

"Sent by my own two feet, indeed, and for the sake of Michael Scot," said the old woman, with some spirit. She eyed us, each in turn. "It seems I've come upon a council of war. Tell me truly, now, before this all goes further; are you with Michael Scot or against him?"

"If he were entirely evil, his heart would be open to me," said Sibylle, "It is not, so I remain neutral, as is just. But I will not allow Frederick to be threatened. He is a good man."

Agnes turned to Nicolai.

"You look like an old hand at traveling. Would you take up with a body if you didn't know where they were bound?"

"Probably not," said he.

"Then you understand me well. You've told me that you're seeking Michael Scot, and you want to know what he's after. Well, we're on the same road so far. But you haven't told me what you'd have of him once you've got him and you know."

"I can speak for no one but myself. For my own part, I discovered Michael Scot by his taking things that I had need of. I would have payment from him."

"Were they yours?"

Nicolai dipped his head, as if she had touched him fencing. "They were of my country. They were needed there," said he.

"So you'll be satisfied if he restores them to your country?"

"It would be a tolerable outcome," said he.

"And what of you, sir?," she said, turning her sharp eyes on me.

"My motives are purely those of curiosity," said I. "I have seen his work. He is an extraordinary scholar, and I am always interested in the career of an extraordinary scholar, especially one trained in my own discipline."

A smile broke out upon her face. "So you're the riddler of the bunch," said she, laughing. "You're curiosity's up nights, worrying, as the lines on your face bear witness. You're a young man to be worrying already over Michael Scot."

"The world is all of my concern," said I, "and I fear what Michael Scot would do with it, were it in the palm of his hand."

"But I tell you true, man, its not him that you should fear, but the black beast riding him. I've come for the sake of his own wild heart, and I'll hear no word against him before I know what he has done and what's been done to him. Hear my tale, all of you, then judge if we can travel together, with the same place in mind."

Nicolai remade his protective circle, for our moving feet had smeared it. We sat around the cunning woman while she told of her dreams and her visions, as well as much of the character of Michael Scot. When she had finished, she looked closely at us.

"I'd be more than glad if we joined forces, for Michael Scot's power has moved on him like an ocean since he was just a lad. If each of you can swear your word that when we try to stop whatever evil is afoot you'll do your best to save him from it as well, then I'll throw my lot in with you and never look back. Whatever skill I have I'll use for you."

"You are the only one of us he is likely to be willing to see. You alone know his strengths and weaknesses," said Nicolai. "It is a fair bargain. I call Perkunas to witness what has been said tonight. I will help save Michael Scot if I can do it without harming what I hold dear."

"I had not thought before now," said I carefully, "that this man might be as much the object of a plot as the author of one. Yet your story is convincingly told. If he is caught in falsehood, it may be my duty as God's servant or my duty as a teacher, but it is my duty all the same to set it right. If you are who you claim to be and your story is true, I am bound by the same duties as you are yourself."

"Very well," said Sibylle. "As long as Frederick and Sicily are not endangered by gentleness to the wizard, I agree."

We talked until dawn, each searching for a theory to explain how Michael Scot could both organize a large working of magic, as Nicolai had seen, yet be controlled by another, as Agnes' dream had shown.

"If he is inhabited by some spirit, it would explain the circumstances," I suggested.

"A man who is not master of his own spirit cannot master the spirit of another," said Nicolai, as if this were a basic rule of logic. "The magus said he was summoned by Michael Scot. If he were summoned by another in the flesh of Michael Scot, he would have named the true summoner instead. The call he answered cares nothing for the flesh."

"But magi cannot be summoned like spirits," said I. "Perhaps you spoke to some spirit that wished to deceive you. I have spoken extensively with members of the Order concerning their nature, and they have made convincing argument against such a possibility."

"Of course they have," said Nicolai, "they are much given to expounding their own greatness." He smiled a small smile, and I believed him. "Once I felt his trace upon the magus, I could recognize the same mark on the horses. I felt this same mark on a ship's captain yesterday. There is no mistake."

"Then I'll speak with the captain, if he hasn't left port." Agnes seemed sure he would confide in her.

"I sent a friend last night to check the ship. It was full of arms. Forgive the ignorance of a foreigner, but these lands seem too full of farms and peasants to make war upon. Luckily, however, the ship ran upon a shoal in the night and filled with water." Nicolai smiled faintly.

We agreed to sleep for a few hours. Though we spread our cloaks within the circle, my mind, disobedient to my will, saw spirits with septic bodies each time I closed my eyes. I sat up to say the Rosary. Not far from me, Sibylle de Bourgogne sat in prayer as I had seen hermits sit, eyes closed, untouched by earthly troubles, her face utterly at peace. When the Rosary was said, I began to build a work that would warn us if Michael Scot sent out a spell of inquiry. I worked in silence, but Agnes' ears were quick.

"What charm do you make, friend?," she whispered. "Perhaps I have a few herbs to aid your work."

"Though Nicolai's circle will keep out airy spirits, it seems Michael Scot has both Natural Magic and the knowledge of the cunning folk as well. I would know if he sends a spell against us. Since he was able to block all my attempts at inquiry with Natural Magic, and then send a spirit that found me, I must assume he knows some skills in this area of which I am ignorant. For that reason, I do not think I can keep him from inquiring of us without alerting him to my activities. However, I can at least make sure we know if he tries."

"God helps those who help themselves," said Agnes, with a smile. "I have a bit of something in my pack to make the work go easier." She brought dried Conium from her pouch of herbs. They were plants of virtue, rich with vis. When the work was complete, I felt a little easier in my mind. As I put the finished work about my neck, Sibylle raised her head.

"Sleep, children. I will not allow you to come to harm."

Agnes looked up to retort, I am sure, that she could help keep the watch, but sat still instead. I followed her gaze. Sibylle de Bourgogne was transfigured in my sight. It seemed at that moment reasonable for her to be no earthly creature, like a linen-draped saint at Cologne, carved perfectly in some incorruptible and ancient wood.

I must have moved to examine her more closely, for she drifted away with a faint, disinterested smile. "Touch me not. Fear not. Michael Scot has no power over me. I will keep the watch."

After we had slept, Agnes and I went to the docks to search for the captain. Unfortunately, the sailors were too familiar with the habits of the wind to believe the grounding of a single ship by a purposeful wind an accident. After their custom, they had decided the captain was bad luck and exiled him from the port. I feared our questions would arouse suspicion, but Agnes' skills were extraordinary.

In some way I could not detect, she allowed them to see she was a cunning-woman. From that moment, she could do no wrong. Sailors trust their lives to God each day, but each one we met was eager for any earthly advantage. In exchange for charms and drinks to make them sure of grip, quick of eye, or free from scurvy, they told her everything they knew. The ship had been loaded in King Frederick's name, so there was no evidence against Michael Scot. Yet Sibylle seemed sure he was responsible. His influence over the king, apparently, is very strong.

At nightfall we gathered again at the house of Sibylle de Bourgogne. Agnes brought the fish the sailors had given us for supper, but Sibylle would not eat. Again, Nicolai drew his circle to protect us from airy spirits, and again Sibylle kept the watch. None of us could persuade her to sleep, either.

That night, I woke in complete darkness. A hand had touched me, just below the throat where my spell lay hidden. It did not threaten, but probed carefully, like the hand of a chirurgeon testing the soundness of my bones. Michael Scot was making an inquiry. The sensation passed. I did not think he had noticed Sibylle at all. In the morning, we sat down to eat, and I told the others what had happened.

"I doubt," said I, "that we can make an effective force if we do not know what Michael Scot is doing, or how. Yet, the longer we wait, the more he can learn of us."

"We are running out of time. Let us go to Sicily." Nicolai seemed eager to face the danger, even if it was not known.

"If we choose to try our luck, I know a captain who would take us…" Agnes leaned back suddenly in her chair, then fell upon the floor like a stone. I reached her quickly. I put my ear to her chest. Her heart beat, regular and strong. She breathed well, though her face was marked by fear. "She has no sign of sickness or congestion of the heart. I don't know what is wrong."

Sibylle touched her forehead, gently. "No evil is within her."

"Nicolai, could it be a spirit?"

"She is within the circle. Only your Satans would appear within it. Sibylle would notice if it was a Satan, yes?"

Agnes opened her eyes and spoke for a moment in a strange tongue.

"Latin, please, German, or Langue d'Oc," I said.

"I'm sorry, gentlemen. Forgive me, my lady de Bourgogne. The good people are not ones to wait their turn for speaking." She seemed calm, though her face was marked both with sadness and with grief. "They have given me counsel."

"Can you tell us of it?"

She closed her eyes. "They have no understanding of our weakness, that we are mortal and have hearts to break. It does no good for all of us to bear the weight. Know only this: if we go blind to face the beast and Michael Scot, we will none of us return alive."

For a moment we all sat in silence. Then Nicolai let his breath out slowly, and stood with the air of one who has made his decision.

"I have the means to solve the problem. Please help me clear a space in the center of the floor, and then shut yourselves in another room. Whatever happens, do not come out until daylight."

"What do you mean to do?"

"If you know nothing of this, you will be completely safe."

Sibyl's face clouded. "I am afraid I cannot allow you bring anything evil into this house," she said softly.

Nicolai laughed, but the sound was short and bitter. "You are a Christian holy woman after all, always suspecting your Satans in everything. Do not worry. I have no need to bring such creatures."

"Nicolai," said Agnes, "I know you'd never be thinking of talking to demons, but the last time you followed your head, you told nobody about it. You sent a man packing who could have told me something of use. I'm slow but sure in my ways, for my skills take time. If you keep the path dark to me, man, I'm likely to trip over something. If you want my help, I've got to know what we're about before it comes knocking at the door."

Nicolai sighed. "There are spirits who know secrets. Whatever Michael Scot is doing, he has hidden it from both ordinary and magical inquiry. He has made it a great secret. If I bring a spirit who knows great secrets, it will know."

I spoke then. "Why do you want us to leave? I have never seen such a spirit, and I would be glad to learn its nature."

"That is why I want you to leave." Nicolai's eyes were angry. "They are dangerous. Their power is only in secrets. They hate to tell, for every telling makes them less. If you learn its secrets, it will want to kill you. I will have to bargain with it for the secret of Michael Scot's plan. That will be difficult and dangerous enough. The danger should be confined to me, for I understand how to deal with it. If you want to stay, you must have nothing to do with the spirit and try to learn nothing of it. You must act as if you do not even know it is there."

"The good folk also have their manners, and truly, those are as far from our own as the manners of the spirits. I've known many a man and woman of their people whose anger is as hard to risk. I know what I'm doing, and I'm going to stay." Agnes' voice was firm.

"If the spirit attacks you," said Sibylle, "you will need my help."

"If Michael Scot detects your activity," I said, "we should be together. None of us is powerful enough to face his work alone."

"Very well. It is against my better judgment. If you value our goals and your lives, you will abide by the instructions I have given you." Nicolai turned back to the wooden floor, where he had begun to draw a complicated pattern in black chalk.

The room took some time to prepare. Nicolai had us shutter the windows with heavy cloth, and press rags beneath the doors. The room grew still and airless. When he had finished his preparations, he turned to us.

"Remember, you must ignore the spirit utterly. You must allow no light into the room. You must stay inside the circle, but you will not be able to see the circle. Therefore, do not move. Keep your eyes closed. Do not speak." His voice was tense. Once he had extinguished the lights, we stood in utter darkness and silence.

We stood for a long time. At first I thought the change in the room was a trick of my senses, grown uncertain from long straining for the slightest sight or sound. In the darkness, there seemed to grow a greater darkness, but it was visible only at the edges of my vision. When I looked at it, it was gone. The air seemed to fill with half-heard whispers, sounds that could have been merely the movement of humors in my own body. When I listened closely, these too retreated. Nicolai began to speak, strange unrecognizable sounds almost too soft to hear. Did a voice respond, or was there only an echo in the room? The question began to prey upon my mind.

Upon reflection, I have come to believe that whatever was in the room with us had an influence upon the mind. Nicolai later confirmed that such spirits seek always to create more secrets, and further uncertainty in the minds of men. I cannot otherwise explain my actions. I know that I began to speculate upon whatever was within the room. I thought perhaps Nicolai had been deceived, and his attempt was unsuccessful, leaving us to stand motionless in that airless darkness for an unknown time, for we could not see the coming of dawn. Then I thought perhaps that Michael Scot had sent a spirit, deceiving us, and we were standing like sheep awaiting slaughter. These thoughts I could control. It was the understanding that what was within the room might be exactly what Nicolai had named, a spirit whose joy was to hide knowledge from the eyes and mind, that moved me to action. I had among my possessions a stone, which could be looked through to aid the powers of perception. I slipped it quietly from my robes, and held it to my eyes. I wished to know the face of my enemy.

I almost saw it clearly. But I must have moved forward in my attempt, for Nicolai's hands closed upon my shoulders and held me still. There is a technique for feeding medicine to animals and children, which takes advantage of the instinct to swallow in order to breathe. Agnes was very skilled in this technique, as well as in the brewing of sleeping potions. I discovered these facts by direct experience at this time.

When I awoke, daylight shone into the room.

"We have our answer," said Sibylle. "Michael Scot is in league with a demon."

"He's made no pact." Agnes looked up angrily. "The evil thing came to him in the guise of a spirit, talked to him of power with a silver tongue. He doesn't even know what he's dealing with. He's always had a weakness for quick gain."

I sat up. "What prize was he offered?"

Nicolai came into the room. "The Satan told him it could disguise him as King Frederick, so perfectly that all would be deceived into believing he had not just the King's shape, but his voice, his knowledge, his manners and his ways. I know of no lesser spirit that can do this. Michael Scot should have known this also."

"Someone who seeks power over the spirits of the earthly world would easily be tempted by demons. Their coin is power over earthly things," said Sibylle.

"That is a myth. We are no closer to Satans than you are yourself. Your own religion is to blame. It takes a strong will and ambition to master spirits. If my will is strong enough, my gods will come to speak with me. For an ambitious Christian like Michael Scot, you offer only Satans and more Satans. A hungry man will eat spoiled food if no better can be had." Nicolai's mood was black. For the first time in many days, I saw that he was truly a foreigner in this land.

"It does no good to fight each other," said Agnes. "We are already agreed to take tomorrow's ship to Sicily. Tell him the rest."

"King Frederick is both king of Sicily and Holy Roman Emperor, yet he does not control Rome. It seems the arms are for its conquest."

"God in Heaven. He's going to war with the pope?"

"Only if he succeeds in impersonating King Frederick, with the aid of the Satan. This we have to prevent. There is one difficulty." Nicolai looked uncomfortable.

"Only one?" said I.

"I had to bargain for the knowledge that the spirit gave to the four of us. The Lucifugum do not give up secrets gladly, and this one was angry because of your curiosity. The only way I was able to get the information was to convince it that we would find out ourselves, even without its help. I told it that if it did not tell us, when we found out we would tell all the world. Its secret would be gone."

"Nicolai, what was the bargain?"

"With the knowledge we now have, we can stop Michael Scot. But the spirit's secret will remain a secret. We are forbidden to tell what we know of his plan to a living soul."

Using the Story of Michael Scot

This story gives storyguides the chance to see how hedge magic fits into Mythic Europe. If you wish, you can use this story as the jumping-off point for a variety of adventures in your saga, to introduce hedge magic to your players.

Adventure #1

Sibylle de Bourgogne's friend, Elaine, received her letter. She has not heard from Sibylle for the season specified, and has now gone seeking help. She goes to the player characters' covenant—one that she feels sure is free from Michael Scot's influence. She shares the contents of the letter with them, as well as the information that her mistress is an ascetic. For that reason, she says, she has gone to other magicians for help.

Elaine is a strong-willed woman, familiar with diplomatic finesse, and determined to save her friend. She is certain that Sibylle's suspicions are vitally important. If necessary, she invents "secret information" that Sibylle supposedly told her, making up anything she thinks would make the covenant more interested in helping. Her estimation of what kinds of problems would interest the covenant are extremely accurate.

Adventure #2

Sibylle de Bourgogne's letter to Elaine was stolen by a petty thief who believed it contained money. Finding it empty of gold, he had it read by a document reader at the local market. Its references to magic frightened him. It frightened him further when the document reader turned up dead. The demon using Michael Scot has discovered the existence of the letter, and is attempting to have everyone who has read it killed. The thief fled, still carrying the letter.

Finding a murderous spirit on his trail, the thief goes to the characters' covenant, begging for help from the magical menace. He believes the letter has some kind of malevolent magic on it, and wants to give it away to magicians. If they can handle it, great. If not, maybe the spirit will want them instead of him, and he won't have the deaths of "normal" people on his conscience.

Adventure #3

Roger Glendower has not heard from Agnes in many days. He is concerned and afraid. He knows someone in the covenant, or has had some positive report of them from a friend of his who does. He goes to the covenant with the story he was told by Agnes and descriptions of Sibylle de Bourgogne and Albertus. The characters are asked to trace what has happened to Agnes. Payment can be made for this service in money or in odd items from his personal cabinet of curiosities.

Character Statistics

Sibylle de Bourgogne

Sibylle grew up as an ordinary girl of noble birth. In 1149 she was married to Roger II, king of Sicily. Exposure to Roger II's court, full of wizards, Muslims, Jews, and scholars of all varieties kindled her interest in philosophy and religion. When Roger died in 1154 Sibylle retired from court life and devoted herself to studies.

In time, and with training from a wandering holy-man who stayed at court for a time, Sibylle became an ascetic. Since that time she has lived at court in Sicily. Her eccentricities and unworldliness have lead most at court of avoid her, though she does attend some court functions.

Many of the servants consider her a holy-woman, seeking her advice when they are troubled. In general, she is ignored by the other nobles at court, but occasionally they too seek her advice when other avenues fail.

Agnes

At first glance, Agnes seems to be merely an elderly herbalist from the Scottish Lowlands. However, those who know her realize she is much more. An extremely talented cunning-woman, Agnes is also widely traveled and well educated. She has numerous friends all over Mythic Europe and knows about a great many matters.

Sibylle de Bourgogne

Age: 94 (Apparent Age 41)

Characteristics: Int +2, Per +3, Pre +1, Com −1, Str −1, Sta +1, Dex 0, Qik 0

Size: 0

Personality Traits: Unworldly +5, Honest +3

Reputations: Eccentric 4, at court in Sicily; Holy 2, among Sicilians

Purity: 4

Weapon/Attack	Init	Atk	Dfn	Dam
Brawl*		−2	−6	−6	−1

*Sibylle has the Noncombatant Flaw, so only engages in combat in self-defense, and only then if sorely pressed. She rolls three extra botch dice in combat.

Soak: +1

Fatigue: −2

Fatigue levels: OK, 0, −1, −3, −5, Unconscious

Body levels: OK, 0, −1, −3, −5, Incapacitated

Virtues & Flaws: Protection +3 (the court of Sicily), Educated +1, Well-Known +1 (Holy), Prestigious Family +1 (Widow of Roger II, king of Sicily), Social Handicap −1 (Blunt), Noncombatant −3

Abilities: Artes Liberales 2 (rhetoric), Awareness 2 (dark perils), Charm 4 (those who believe that she is holy), Chirurgy 2 (binding wounds), Church Lore 3 (heresies), Concentration 7 (meditation), Disputatio 3 (theology), Etiquette 3 (Sicilian court), Leadership 3 (lead by example), Medicine 2 (physician), Sense Holy/Unholy 5 (in people), Scribe Latin 4, Speak Arabic 4, Speak Greek 4, Speak Italian 5, Speak Latin 5, Theology 2 (heresy)

Agnes the Cunning-woman

Age: 65 (Apparent Age 45)

Characteristics: Int +3, Per +4, Pre 0, Com +1, Str –1, Sta 0, Dex –1, Qik –2

Size: 0

Personality Traits: Practical +4, Loyal +3

Reputations: Wise 3, among surrounding peasants; Kindly 3, among those who have heard of her "professionally"

Virtues & Flaws: Clear Thinker +1, Common Sense +1, Educated +1, Great Perception +2, Social Contacts +1 (among scholars and hedge wizards), Well-Traveled +1, Fragile Constitution –1, Oversensitive –1 (poor manners), Lame –2

Weapon/Attack	Init	Atk	Dfn	Dam
Brawl	–3	–3	–3	0

Soak: 0

Fatigue: 0

Fatigue levels: OK, 0, –1, –3, –5, Unconscious

Body levels: OK, 0, –1, –3, –5, Incapacitated

Abilities: Artes Liberales 2 (rhetoric), Awareness 3 (plants and animals), Bargain 3 (peasants), Chirurgy 4 (diagnosis), Craft Bane 4 (misfortune), Craft Charm 5 (health), Faerie Lore 4 (faerie lords), Faerie Sight 3 (regiones), Folk Ken 3 (peasants), Folk Magic 6 (potions), Herbalism 6 (health), Medicine 2 (physician), Scribe English 3, Scribe Latin 3, Speak English 5, Speak Latin 4, Storytelling 2, Survival 3 (forest), Visions 3 (faerie)

For all her knowledge and skill, Agnes behaves like a quiet, humble, and unassuming woman who enjoys gardening and talking with polite visitors from all walks of life.

Nicolai

Nicolai the Spirit Master grew up in a small Lithuanian village. His parents, like many in their village, followed the old pre-Christian religion of the area. Nicolai shares this faith, but is understandably reticent to discuss this fact. When Nicolai was a youth, his village was destroyed by the Christian knights in one of their periodic "crusades" against Baltic pagans.

He became a wanderer, seeking knowledge, power, and fortune. While in Kiev he caught the eye of a wandering merchant who was also a spirit master. Nicolai traveled with him for many years, finally setting out on his own. He has become a successful merchant, using his skill at driving bargains to his advantage. For a price, he will summon airy spirits and magical beasts of all types, but only when it meets with his whim.

Albertus

Albertus is a Dominican who has also gained fame as a natural magician. Born to the Count von Bollstadt, he rejected the privileges of the nobility for a life of scholarship and learning, against the wishes of his family.

Even at his young age he is gaining a reputation as one of the keenest minds in Europe. He has only recently become a Dominican, but has rapidly gained acceptance in their hierarchy—his reputation as a theologian is only surpassed by his reputation as a scholar. Unlike many of his fellows, Albert investigates as much as he studies, and will go to great lengths to explore the interesting stories he hears.

Michael Scot

Michael Scot is one of the most enigmatically famous people in Mythic Europe. On one hand, Scot is widely acclaimed as one of the great magi-

Nicolai the Spirit Master

Age: 40 (Apparent Age 30)

Characteristics: Int +3, Per +3, Pre 0, Com +2, Str +1, Sta 0, Dex –1, Qik 0

Size: 0

Personality Traits: Clever +3, Shrewd +3, Honorable +2

Reputations: Hard Trader 3, Lithuanian areas; Honorable 2, among those who have traded with him;

Virtues and Flaws: Direction Sense +1, Light Sleeper +1, Sharp Ears +1, Well-Traveled +1, Charmed Life +3, Oversensitive –1 (Oppressing the weak), Oversensitive –1 (People who dislike foreigners), Social Handicap –1 (Dour)

Weapon/Attack	Init	Atk	Dfn	Dam
Brawl	+5	+3	+4	+1
Dagger	+6	+4	+6	+3

Soak: +1

Fatigue: +4

Fatigue levels: OK, 0, –1, –3, –5, Unconscious

Body levels: OK, 0, –1, –3, –5, Incapacitated

Abilities: Bargain 5 (airy spirits), Brawl 3 (knife), Charm 4 (customers), Concentration 3 (summoning), Direction Sense 2 (at night), Intrigue 3 (hedge wizards), Folk Ken 3 (customers), Legend Lore 3 (airy spirits), Magic Sensitivity 3 (beasts of virtue), Occult Lore 5 (spirits of sickness), Scribe Latin 1, Second Sight 4 (airy spirits), Single Weapon 3 (ax), Speak Arabic 3, Speak French 2, Speak German 3, Speak Italian 3, Speak Latin 3, Speak Lithuanian 5, Speak Russian 4, Summoning 6 (beasts of virtue), Survival 3 (forest)

Albertus

Age: 27

Characteristics: Int +5, Per +3, Pre 0, Com +2, Str –2, Sta 0, Dex 0, Qik 0

Size: 0

Personality Traits: Curious +4, Wise +2, Stubborn +2

Reputations: Brilliant 2, among scholars across Mythic Europe

Virtues and Flaws: Clear Thinker +1, Strong-Willed +1, Well-Traveled +1, Magister in Artibus +3, Incredible Intelligence +4, Driving Goal –1 (Understand the natural world), Weakness –1 (acquiring knowledge), Overconfident –2

Weapon/Attack	Init	Atk	Dfn	Dam
Brawl	+2	+2	+1	0

Soak: +1

Fatigue: +2

Fatigue levels: OK, 0, –1, –3, –5, Unconscious

Body levels: OK, 0, –1, –3, –5, Incapacitated

Abilities: Alchemy 4 (transformations), Artes Liberales 4 (logic), Philosophiae 5 (spellcrafting), Awareness 2 (urban), Concentration 3 (reading), Disputatio 4 (teaching), Etiquette 2 (scholarly), Lectio 3 (natural magic), Legend Lore 3 (church), Magic Theory 2 (theoretical aspects), Magic Sensitivity 3 (vis), Medicine 2 (anatomy), Scribe Greek 4, Scribe Latin 5, Speak German 5, Speak Italian 3, Speak Latin 5, Speak Greek 3, Theology 4 (history)

cians of the age; on the other, the Order of Hermes dismisses him as a mere hedge wizard. Some say that he allies himself with demons; others that he is one of the greatest men who has ever lived. The learned know that he studied medicine, philosophy, and natural magic. Most who have taught and studied with him sing his praises as a fine scholar. He reads fluent Arabic and has written acclaimed commentaries on Aristotle. Michael Scot is in demand as a magician, an astrologer, and a physician. Most do not know that natural magic is but one of his talents.

Michael Scot is one of the very few to master multiple magical methods. He was trained as a cunning-man as a youth in Scotland. From there he traveled to Padua and learned natural magic. Finally, he learned spirit mastery in the East. Disregarding his vast knowledge, the Order of Hermes maintains that he is a trumped up hedge wizard. This reputation may be in part because Michael Scot avoids the Order when he can, because he has no desire to join an organization that would limit his influence and his power.

Michael Scot has recently become Frederick II's court wizard. He received this appointment by winning a competition against a dozen other hedge wizards whom Frederick invited to compete for the title. Since Frederick holds the titles of both king of Sicily and Holy Roman Emperor, Michael Scot has reached a position of great power.

There are many stories told about Michael Scot, most of which he neither confirms nor denies. It is said that he always wears a steel cap because he knows he is fated to die from a blow to the head. It is also said that God and the Devil both desire his soul, but only God knows which will get it.

Michael Scot, Court Wizard of Frederick II

Age: 40 (Apparent Age 33)

Characteristics: Int +3, Per +3, Pre +4, Com +2, Str +1, Sta +2, Dex +1, Qik 0

Size: 0

Personality Traits: Power-hungry +3, Brilliant +3

Reputations: Great Magician 4, throughout the lands of Frederick II; Diabolist 2, among some clerics and magi; Hedge Wizard 2, Order of Hermes

Virtues and Flaws: Strong-Willed +1, Light Sleeper +1, Famous +2 (Great and powerful wizard), Patron +2 (Frederick II), Great Presence +2, Bad Reputation –1 (Suspicions of diabolism), Dark Secret –1 (Allied with a demon), Oversensitive –1 (Insults), Overconfident –2

Weapon/Attack	Init	Atk	Dfn	Dam
Brawl	+4	+4	+3	+1

Soak: +2

Fatigue: +5

Fatigue levels: OK, 0, –1, –3, –5, Unconscious

Body levels: OK, 0, –1, –3, –5, Incapacitated

Abilities: Alchemy 5 (transformations), Artes Liberales 4 (rhetoric), Philosophiae 5 (spellcrafting), Brawl 3 (fist), Charm 4 (clergy), Chirurgy 3 (binding wounds), Concentration 3 (study), Craft Bane 5 (misfortune), Craft Charm 5 (wealth), Intrigue 3 (plotting), Etiquette 2 (nobility), Folk Magic 5 (banes), Herbalism 5 (poisons), Legend Lore 3 (hedge wizardry), Magic Sensitivity 4 (stones of virtue), Magic Theory 2 (Mentem), Medicine 4 (apothecary), Occult Lore 4 (demons), Summoning 6 (spirits of sickness), Scribe Arabic 3, Scribe Greek 3, Scribe Latin 4, Second Sight 4 (airy spirits), Speak Arabic 3, Speak English 5, Speak French 4, Speak Greek 4, Speak Italian 4, Speak Latin 5, Visions 2 (faerie)

Chapter 3
Hedge Wizardry

The rules in this chapter allow for the creation of hedge wizards in game terms, either as player characters or non-player characters. Hedge wizards can be entertaining and rewarding characters, and most sagas should have little trouble incorporating them.

There are two ways to play a character who is a hedge wizard—the option that is right for your saga depends on your tastes. The first option is to allow players to create regular companions that have some of the abilities and powers of hedge wizards. In this case, hedge wizard special abilities are bought as Virtues and paid for with Flaws. However, hedge wizards who are generated as companions will be limited in both power and versatility. They represent the lower range of hedge wizard power and ability.

It is also possible to play a hedge wizard who is fully trained, with the potential to challenge the greatest hedge wizards in Mythic Europe. Such characters are generated as mystic companions. Mystic companions are significantly less powerful than full Hermetic magi, but they are more powerful than ordinary companions.

This creates a dilemma. Should a mystic companion occupy a player's companion slot, or his magus slot? Each troupe should decide for itself, considering such factors the power levels of other characters in the troupe, the amount of game time usually spent on laboratory activities (because seasonal sagas leave non-magi with little to do between adventures), and the importance of membership in the Order of Hermes in the campaign. It is recommended that mystic companions occupy the magus slot, but each troupe should make the final decision for itself.

Creating Mystic Companions

Mystic companions are created much like other companions—most steps follow the regular rules for companion creation found in the **Ars Magica** Fourth Edition rulebook. The only significant differences lie in mystic companions' special training, and in the Abilities they begin the game with. Again, it is important to note that mystic companions are far more powerful than standard companions. Troupes should carefully consider whether mystical companions occupy a player's companion or magus slot.

When creating a mystic companion, the player must choose one of the four types of hedge wizard: cunning-man, natural magician, spirit master, or ascetic. At the troupe's option, new traditions of hedge wizardry may also be chosen; see "Other Traditions" on page 56. The character gains all of the capabilities detailed in the appropriate description. He also gains the listed Abilities, in addition to the standard companion Ability to Speak Own Language at a score of 5. Finally, instead of spending the companion's standard (age x 2) experience points on Abilities, mystic companion hedge wizards spend (age +10).

Mystic companions are generated in all other ways like standard companions.

Companions as Hedge Wizards

If you would prefer to generate a standard companion with some hedge wizard capabilities, simply select from among the new Virtues found beginning on page 54. There are no other changes to the companion-generation process.

I WILL TAKE ANY STUDENT, rich or poor, noble or common, and I've seen some of each in my time. All you need is a touch of the sight and a keen eye for the world around you. But, that said, don't be thinking me an easy teacher. You will work as hard as if you had gone to the new university in the city, or even to that dank pile of stone where the blind and pompous Magi live. Yes, I've been to those places. The city does not suit me, and the magi can't tell mandrake from carrots. I may look like a simple old man, but I've traveled further than you, and had students trickier than I expect you'll ever be. If you truly want to learn, and are willing to work hard to do so, you are welcome to stay. If not, don't be wasting both our time.

–Jervais the Cunning-man to a prospective student

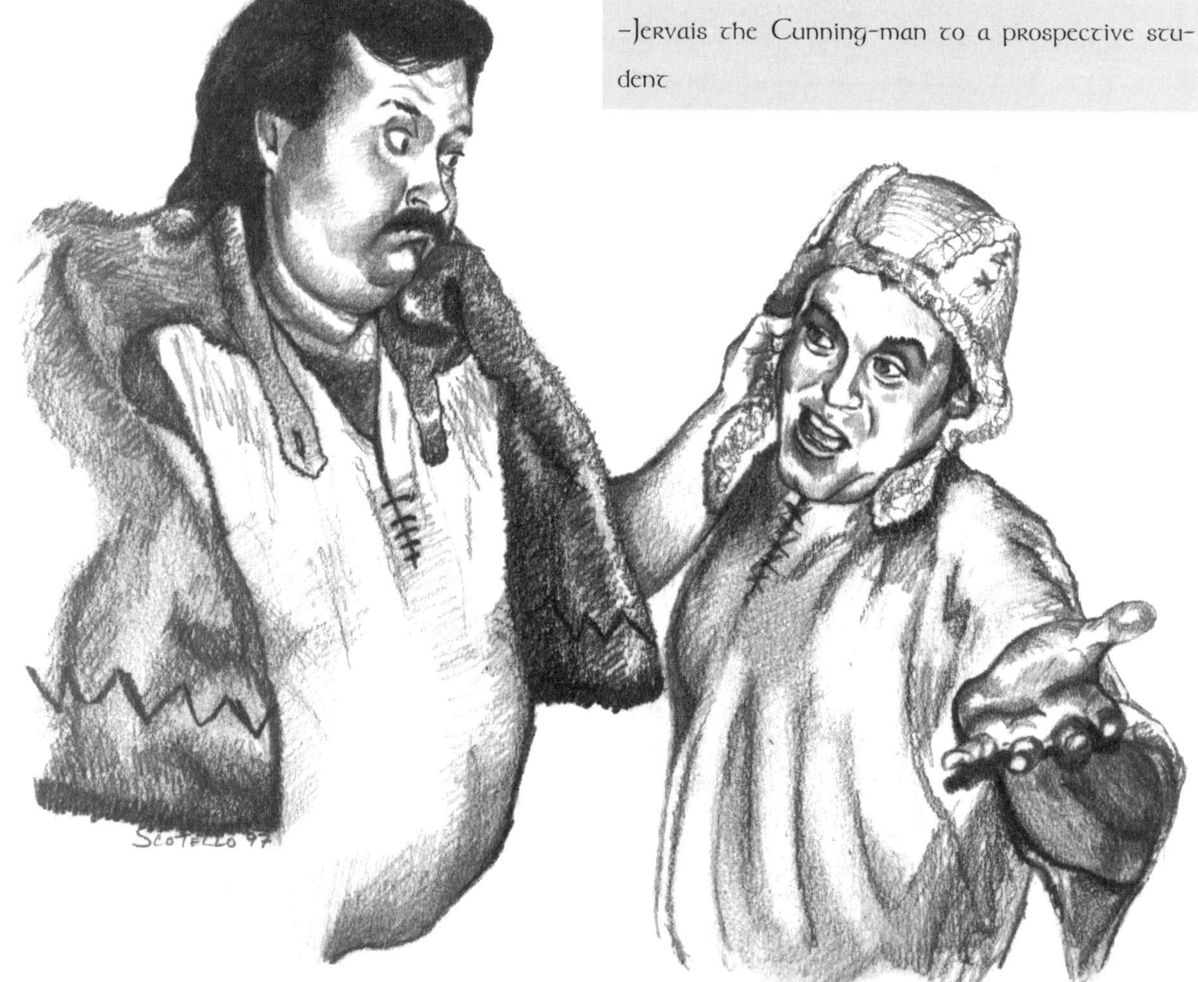

Joining the Order of Hermes

When they begin play, mystic companions will not be powerful enough to be eligible to join the Order of Hermes. However, as play continues, some mystic companions may wish to join the Order. In general, to join the Order a mystic companion must raise his primary ability to at least eight. In addition, the character must also be able to speak and read Latin with moderate fluency (a minimum Speak Latin 4 and Scribe Latin 3). Mystic companions who meet these conditions and who are sponsored by a member of House Ex Miscellanea may join the Order of Hermes, barring any political problems.

Many hedge wizards will not want to join the Order, and this is perfectly logical. In general, hedge wizards are beneath the notice of most Hermetic Magi, and so they will not normally be asked to join or die. In addition, many hedge wizards make their living working for mundanes, and joining the Order precludes such a possibility. Hedge wizard characters should think carefully before deciding to become part of the Order.

Auras and Hedge Wizardry

Because of the diversity of the exact sources of their power, hedge wizards are affected by auras a little differently than Hermetic magi are. The chart below summarizes how each type of aura affects the activities of each type of hedge wizard. Characters who possess the powers of hedge wizards through possession of an odd Virtue or two rather than wholesale subscription to a given school of hedge wizardry use these modifiers when practicing the abilities of that school. For example, if a Hermetic magus with the Virtue Charm Maker were creating a charm, he would use the aura modifiers listed below rather than those he normally uses when casting Hermetic spells or performing other Hermetic activities.

Hedge Wizard Aura Interaction Table

Hedge Wizard	Power Used			
	Magic	Divine	Faerie	Infernal
Cunning-folk	+ (aura)	– (aura)	+ (aura)	– (aura)
Natural Magicians	+ (aura)	no effect	+ (1/2 aura)	– (aura)
Spirit Masters	+ (aura)	– (1/2 aura)	– (1/2 aura)	– (1/2 aura)
Ascetics	+ (aura)	+ (aura)	+ (aura)	–(aura)

Cunning-folk

Cunning-folk are hedge wizards, generally of rural birth, who specialize in making potions and charms that effect plants, animals, and people. Cunning-folk are also closer to faeries and faerie things than most mortals. As a part of their unique perceptions of things faerie, cunning-folk often have useful visions and dreams.

Though often well-educated and well-traveled, almost all cunning-folk are of low birth. Nobles and wealthy families are more attracted to the expensive paraphernalia of natural magic, and would be scandalized to learn that a relative was learning peasant charms. While this low status is galling to some, it also serves to protect cunning-folk, since they are beneath the notice of both the Order and the higher levels of the Church hierarchy. Except in rare cases where cunning-folk have propagated heresies or pagan practices, priests generally ignore them entirely or make use of their abilities as needed. Monks, nuns, and "uneducated" rural parish priests are occasionally trained cunning-folk, as well.

Cunning-folk are distinguished by the Abilities Craft Charm, Craft Bane, Folk Magic, Herbalism, Faerie Sight, and Visions. They also are able to find and use wild vis. All cunning-folk who are mystic companions start with the following Abilities at no cost. Cunning-folk have a minimum age of 20.

Chirurgy 2

Craft Charm 2

Craft Bane 2

Faerie Lore 3

Faerie Sight 2

Folk Magic 4

Herbalism 4

Visions 2

Herbalism

All cunning-folk are skilled herbalists, adept at making wondrous potions and charms from ordinary materials found in the world around them. Whether they are making curative potions out of the correct mixture of common garden herbs or locating the one magical sprig of clover in a field, cunning-folk are able to use natural material in ways others cannot. Cunning-folk find the ingredients they need for all their magical operations easily and quickly among the common plants, animals, and natural materials around them.

Potions

Cunning-folk can create potions using their skill with Herbalism. Their Lab total for this activity is Intelligence + Herbalism + Herbalism bonuses + Folk Magic + aura of the site where the potion is made. If both magic and faerie auras are present, use only the greatest. Herbalism bonuses are those that are part of the definition of the Herbalism Ability (ArM4, page 41). They include

+5 for poisons, , +5 for antidotes, +5 for healing and health, and +3 for hallucinogens.

These types of potions take a season to create, and should be treated in all ways like ordinary Hermetic potions. They may be created out of ordinary herbs cunning-folk have on hand, and so require no special ingredients. As with hermetic potions multiple doses can be made in a single season if the lab total is high enough. For more details on creating potions see ArM4, page 88-89.

The only exception to the rule that potions require no special ingredients is the case of potions which require the use of vis. When creating a potion which would require vis cunning-folk may use wild vis to make the potion (though they can certainly use regular vis if they choose).

Minor Potions

Cunning-folk can use their Herbalism in smaller and more immediate ways by creating minor potions (or salves, poultices, incenses, etc.) which give bonuses to Abilities. Specific applications are listed below. Minor potions take one hour to create if the cunning-man has a ready supply of herbs and two hours if the herbs must be gathered. Only one dose of a minor potion can be made at a time.

Minor Potions can add to the following Skill and Talent rolls:

- *Awareness:* A potion which sharpens your perceptions and keeps you awake.

- *Animal Handling:* A potion you feed to an animal that makes it more cooperative.

- *Chirurgy:* The chirurgeon does not imbibe the potions and poultices produced. Rather, they are applied directly to the wounded who are treated. The bonus adds to the chirurgeon Ability roll.

- *Carouse:* Potions and herbs to help you keep sober.

- *Concentration:* Potions to help clarify and focus you mind.

- *Second Sight or Faerie Sight:* A potion to change your perceptions.

- *Survival:* potions to enhance your endurance and the nutrition of poor food.

- *Visions:* A mild hallucinogen which adds only to your roll for having visions. You also suffer half the bonus (round up) as a penalty to all mundane perception rolls for the day.

Successful creation of a minor potion requires a roll of 9+ on a stress die + Intelligence + Herbalism (but don't make the roll until the potion is consumed). If this roll succeeds the person drinking the potion may add the maker's Herbalism score (+ any bonuses imparted by the definition of Herbalism) divided by two to the Ability in question for the next full day. If the roll fails the potion has no effect. If the roll botches (use three botch dice), the person drinking the potion becomes ill, and takes the maker's full Herbalism as a penalty to all rolls involving Stamina for the next full day. Double and triple botches either double or triple the penalty, respectively, or have some other effect of the storyguide's devising.

It is possible to create minor potions which purposefully subtract the maker's Herbalism score from any of the listed Abilities. Failures and botches work the same way they do for beneficial potions.

The effects of a minor potion last for a full day. Multiple potions taken for the same Ability during the same day do not have cumulative effects. If two or more potions applying to the same Ability are taken in one day, both potions fail and the subject becomes ill, taking a –3 Stamina penalty for the next full day.

Even taking multiple potions for different Abilities in the same day can be risky. For every minor potion after the first taken in one day, add another botch die when rolling for the effect of the potion. If more than two minor potions are taken in a single day, roll botch dice for every additional potion consumed even if the additional potions are effective. For example, when imbibing his fourth minor potion in a single day, Jervais rolls better than a 9, rendering the potion fully effective. He must now roll six botch dice to see if he suffers from negative effects.

Minor potions do not keep after they are made—they must be used within one full day of being made or they go bad and produce no effect when imbibed. If left sitting for more than a week, they act as botched minor potions when finally consumed.

Wild Vis

Wild vis is a special type of vis only cunningfolk know how to find and use. Some magi speculate that wild vis is in some way linked to faerie power, and that cunning-folk can detect and use it because of their special connection to faerie things. Merinita magi contest this assertion. They argue that if wild vis were faerie in nature, they would be able to detect and use it. Others suggest that wild vis is some sort of proto-vis—that if left alone, wild vis eventually manifests as the raw vis that Hermetic magi can use. In any case, standard Hermetic magi can neither detect nor utilize wild vis as they can detect and use standard raw vis, though they can still benefit from the special abilities that many stones, plants, and animals of virtue possess.

Wild vis occurs only in special minerals, plants or animals. These are called materials of virtue. Some types of materials of virtue are described in Chapter 4, but that list is by no means exhaustive. In fact, most of the wild vis that cunning-folk collect are simply rare herbs like four-leafed clovers which contain a single pawn of wild vis and have no other magical properties.

All materials of virtue contain wild vis. While everyone else (including Hermetic magi) sees only an ordinary creature or object, cunning-folk can see the one oak-leaf in the forest, pebble on the strand, or goat in the herd that contains wild vis. Though wild vis occurs everywhere, it is much more common in certain types of stones, plants, and animals, as well as in faerie or magic auras.

Any item that contains wild vis may be used by a cunning-man for any magical operation he can perform that normally requires standard vis. Wild vis works exactly like normal vis when used in this way, save that wild vis is not associated with Hermetic Arts, as standard vis is. One pawn of wild vis has the same use value as one pawn of standard vis (that is, one measure of wild vis replaces one pawn of regular vis in situations where it can be used).

Gathering small amounts of wild vis takes little time. Because of this, it is possible for cunning-folk to collect wild vis even while they are at work on other projects. If a cunning-man is doing other things, wild vis can be casually gathered at a rate of (Perception + Herbalism + Faerie Sight + Magical or Faerie Aura)/10 pawns per season. If an entire season is spent doing nothing but gathering wild vis, much more can be accumulated— [Perception + Herbalism + Faerie Sight + (3 x Magical or Faerie Aura)]/5 pawns per season. In each case, the storyguide decides what kind of material is found. It should usually be drawn from a common material, native to the region.

Finding a specific magical material is more difficult than simply looking for any local source of wild vis. If such a search is conducted in a casual fashion in a season where other activities are being performed a stress roll + Perception + Herbalism will be required to find a single sample of the desired material. If the search is conducted intensively for a full season the roll is the same, but the chance of success is much higher. Consult the Wild Vis Search Table, below, for target numbers. In either case, for every full 5 points that the total exceeds the target number, one additional measure of the desired material is found.

In order to know about the special properties and uses of a specific magical plant, stone, or animal (Herbalism conveys a knowledge of all useful natural materials), a cunning-man must roll a simple die + Intelligence + Herbalism of 9+. If successful, the cunning-man can also determine if the magical material in question can be found in his vicinity, and if not, where it might be found. Most of the magical materials listed in this book can be found throughout Mythic Europe.

Wild Vis Search Table

Casual Search

Rarity of Material	Target Number
Common	12
Uncommon	15
Rare	18
Very Rare	21

Season-long Search

Rarity of Material	Target Number
Common	6
Uncommon	9
Rare	12
Very Rare	15

Charms and Banes

The most potent power of the cunning-folk is the ability to craft charms and banes. These are small talismans that can be made to bring good or ill, and can be made to affect any living thing.

Charms and banes come in two types, lesser and greater. Lesser charms and banes function for a limited time, described by a duration, which is describes the amount of time from its creation that the charm or bane remains magical, and a number of uses, the number of times the effect it provides is generated. Possible durations are one day, one week, or one month; number of uses can be once, three times, or continuously during the duration. If all of a charm or bane's uses have not been expended by the end of the duration, they are lost. Greater charms last until dispelled or destroyed, functioning continually as they are carried.

In general, charms and banes grant the benefits of Virtues and the detriments of Flaws. They are limited to those Virtues and Flaws that make sense. For example, it would be possible to develop a Knack or Exceptional Talent. Suddenly gaining a Diabolic Upbringing is absurd. The effects of Hermetic Virtues and Flaws can't be duplicated without the specific permission of the troupe or storyguide; such charms and banes could easily become abusive, and the decision to allow them should not be taken lightly. Some charms can also impart bonuses to Characteristics and Abilities.

Charms and banes may not affect non-living targets, bestow the effects of divinely- or infernally-granted Virtues or Flaws, cause retroactive effects (like grant or remove the effects of Virtues or Flaws that deal with character background).

Cunning-folk can also make charms of longevity. Such charms are always greater charms, and must be worn or carried constantly to be effective. Like longevity potions, they cease to be effective if the target gains an affliction, gains points in an existing affliction, or gains a Decrepitude point. When a longevity charm fails, a new one must be constructed. Longevity charms are not cumulative with longevity potions. Only the charm or potion with the greatest benefit functions, while the other has no effect. If the greater of the two should fail, however, the other remains in effect until it fails on its own.

All charms and banes are made specifically for one target. If someone other than the intended target carries a charm or bane it has no effect. To function, charms and banes must be in contact with their targets. Blessing a field (which is considered a living thing for these purposes) is possible by burying a charm in the field. To bestow a blessing on a person you must give him the charm to carry. Likewise for banes—to curse someone you must either find some way to give him the cursed charm, or place it somewhere close, such as in his home or under his bed.

No one may be affected by more than three lesser charms and three greater charms at once. Likewise, no one may be affected by more than three lesser banes and three greater banes at once. If more than this number are carried only three of each variety will function, usually the first three that were picked up.

Charms and banes are not cumulative. In cases where two or more similar charms or banes are carried the one with the largest bonus (or penalty) functions and the others do not. For example, if a character were carrying two charms, one imparting a +2 knack with swords and the other a +3 knack with swords, only the +3 charm would function. The same thing happens if a charm and bane are both placed on the same person. A +1 Intelligence charm and a –2 Intelligence bane working against one another would result in a –2. If a charm and bane of equal magnitude are at work, they cancel each other out for no effect.

Lesser charms and banes take one day's work to create. Such charms and banes are made out of readily available natural materials such as sprigs of herbs, colored thread, sticks, and bones. These charms and banes can be made as large as desired, but must be at least the size of large grape. Some cunning-folk are said to live in dwellings that are themselves enormous charms.

Greater charms and banes take a full season to make. They are exactly the same as lesser charms and banes in terms of limits on material and size,

but greater charms and banes also require vis. One pawn of vis is required for every ten points (or fraction thereof) of the total ease factor. For example, if a charm had an ease factor of 27 it would require 3 pawns of vis. As with all of their magical operations, cunning-folk can use wild vis is the place of standard vis.

Successfully creating a charm requires a stress roll + Intelligence + Craft Charm or Craft Bane + Folk Magic + Herbalism + faerie or magical aura. The base ease factor for making greater or lesser charms and banes is 12 and is modified by a number of factors.

Example Lesser Charm

Juliet is a young woman in a peasant village who is in love with Alain the miller's son. Alain takes no notice of Juliet. Juliet goes to Gerard, the local-cunning-man, and explains the situation.

Gerard explains that he can make a charm for Juliet so that Alain will be attracted to her the next time they talk. The rest is up to her. He asks

Charm Ease Factor Modifiers

Base Ease Factor: 12

Effect	Ease Factor Modifier
Increase a Characteristic	+ (7 x increase)
Increase an Ability	+ (3 x increase)
Add a Virtue effect	+ (7 x Virtue Score)
Remove a Flaw effect	+ (7 x Flaw Score)
Longevity Charm (for self)	+ (3 x subtraction from aging rolls)
Longevity Charm (for other)	+ (5 x subtraction from aging rolls)

For lesser charms, divide the total modifier by 2 and round up. After this division, apply modifiers from the Lesser Charm and Bane Duration Table based on the desired duration. The result (plus the base ease factor of 12) is the final ease factor.

for a chicken in return. Juliet pays him the chicken, and Gerard spends a day making the charm.

Gerard's ease factor is 12 (base) + [7 (Produce effect of Venus' Blessing) ÷ 2 (because this is a lesser charm)], or 16. Gerard decides that it will remain effective for one week (+1), but will only be of use during the next conversation that Juliet and Alain have (−1). The final ease factor remains at 16. Gerard rolls a 4. His score, then, is 4 (the roll) + 2 (his Intelligence) + 3 (his Craft Charm score) + 4 (his Folk Magic score) + 5 (his Herbalism score), for a total of 18. The lesser charm he has made will give Juliet the +1 Virtue Venus' Blessing the next time she talks with Alain (as long as that happens before a week passes), for the duration of the conversation.

Example Greater Charm

Finn, a farmer, has suffered a damaging series of blights. He seeks a way to protect his crops from these blights. Finn has heard of Rose the cunning-woman, so he goes to her and asks for a charm to protect his crops. Rose says she can make such a charm. Finn is overjoyed, and Rose tells him it will take her a season and the price will be two cows and two goats or the goods to barter for them. After much haggling Finn agrees.

Rose sets to work. The storyguide decides that the Virtue to be imparted is Immunity, and assigns a value of +3. Her ease factor, then, is 12 (base) + 21 (she is instilling a +3 Virtue), or 33.

She spends a season hard at work, uses 4 pawns of vis to make the charm permanent, and rolls a 7. Her total is 7 (her roll) + 3 (her Intelligence) + 5 (her Craft Charm score) + 6 (her Folk Magic score) + 6 (her Herbalism score) + 6 (from the Faerie Aura she lives in), for a total of 33. She succeeds. The next season Finn returns to collect his charm and pays Rose the agreed upon cows and goats and goes off to bury the charm in his fields.

Example Lesser Bane

Paul, the only son of a local lord, has been harassing the people of his father's village. He has

Bane Ease Factor Modifiers

Base Ease Factor: 12

Effect	Ease Factor Modifier
Cap an Ability at its current level	+3
Rolls in a single Ability are always zero	+14
Rolls in a single Ability always botch	+21
Reduce a characteristic	+ (7 x reduction)
Add the effects of a Flaw	+ (7 x Flaw Score)
Remove the effects of a Virtue	+ (7 x Virtue Score)

For lesser banes, divide the total modifier by 2 and round up. After this division, apply modifiers from the Lesser Charm and Bane Duration Table based on the desired duration. The result (plus the base ease factor of 12) is the final ease factor.

Lesser Charm and Bane Duration Table

Duration	Ease Factor Modifier
Day	+0
Week	+1
Month	+2

Number of Uses	Ease Factor Modifier
One	−1
Three	+0
Continuous	+1

Cunning-folk Summary of Formulae

Brew Potions
Lab total = Intelligence + Herbalism + Herbalism bonus + Folk Magic + aura

Gather Wild Vis (working on other tasks)
(Perception + Herbalism + Faerie Sight + Magical or Faerie Aura)/10 pawns per season

Gather Wild Vis (dedicated season)
[Perception + Herbalism + Faerie Sight + (3 x Magical or Faerie Aura)]/5 pawns per season

Minor Potion
stress die + Intelligence + Herbalism; ease factor 9+

Craft Charm/Craft Bane
stress die + Intelligence + Craft Charm or Craft Bane + Folk Magic + Herbalism + aura

trampled fields, scared livestock, and most recently has beaten senseless an old man who got in his way. The lord is old and takes no notice of Paul's behavior. The villagers worry about how things will be when Paul is their lord.

Elsie, the local cunning-woman, has watched Paul grow up and knows he is full of hatred and malice. Unwilling to see Paul become lord of the village, she plans for his demise. She makes a bane so that the next time he gallops on his horse he will take what she hopes will be a fatal fall (that is, he will botch the next riding roll he makes when galloping).

Her base ease factor is 12 (base) + [21 (always botch) ÷ 2 (lesser bane)], or 23. This charm will remain effective for a month (+2), and function only once (–1). The final ease factor is 24.

Elsie spends a day making the bane, and rolls a 3. Her total, then, is 3 (the roll) + 3 (her Intelligence) + 4 (her Craft Bane score) + 5 (her Folk Magic score) + 6 (her Herbalism score) + 3 (from her Aura), for a total of 24. She succeeds.

Elsie talks to the stable-boy (who has no love for Paul), and convinces him to slip the charm into Paul's saddle when he is polishing it.

Natural Magicians

Natural magicians use the magic found within the natural world—in stones, herbs, animals, and the alignments of the stars—to produce a wide variety of magical effects. Unlike cunning-folk, who tap hidden properties inherent in stones, plants, and animals to affect other living things, natural magicians use the disciplines of natural philosophy to create special stones, plants, and animals that, when used in combination with one another, can potentially make any magical effect they desire.

While some natural magicians actively study the natural world, most seek out the knowledge of the ancients in order to gain understanding of the

magic in the world. Natural magicians are both highly trained scholars and skilled practitioners of magic.

Most natural magicians belong to the Magister in Artibus social class. They are considered to possess this Virtue at no cost, and skip the Companion Social Class selection stage that other companions go through. Even those that may not be able to possess the formal title Magister in Artibus (because they are female, or have other social conflicts) have had similar training. Whether a given natural magician possesses the title Magister in Artibus, he may spend an extra 21 experience points on Academic Knowledges and Skills during character creation, and may select the Further Education Virtue. As universities spread across the face of Mythic Europe so do natural magicians. They may be found in Cambridge and in Paris, in Toledo and in Padua. Wherever there are scholars and books there are natural magicians.

Natural magic is gaining rapid acceptance from the Church. It is seen by most progressive clergy as one more of God's many gifts to humankind. Even clerics who look askance at the magics of the Order of Hermes often accept that an amethystus can aid them in keeping a clear head.

All natural magician mystic companion characters start with the following Abilities at no cost. Natural magicians have a minimum age of (27 − Intelligence).

Alchemy 3

Artes Liberales 3

Civil and Canon Law 1

Disputatio 2

Lectio 2

Magic Sensitivity 2

Scribe Latin 2

Speak Latin 4

Philosophiae 3

Natural Alchemy

Potions

Natural magicians may create potions using the same rules as Hermetic magi, save that their Lab total is Intelligence + Alchemy + Philosophiae + aura + any alchemical bonuses. Alchemical bonuses are +5 for poisons, +4 for antidotes, +3 for healing and health, and +2 for transformations (as listed in ArM4, page 40). These potions act just like Hermetic potions. If the effect desired requires vis the natural magician must acquire it normally.

Natural magicians use vis in potions just like Hermetic magi do, by adding extra vis to the brew in order to boost range or increase Lab total. Like magi, they must use Art-specific vis.

Transformations

In addition to brewing potions, natural magicians can use their alchemical knowledge to enchant materials, bringing out the materials' magical properties. For example, a natural magician could take an ordinary amethyst and turn it into a magical Amethystus. Natural magicians can transform both plants and stones (but not animals) in this way. For detailed information on the types of magical materials that exist, see Chapter 4.

To bring about such a transformation it is necessary to spend an entire season preparing the material. Among other procedures, the raw material must be boiled in a special solution, which must include one pawn of vis, which can be associated with any Art. Natural magicians may not engage any other activities in a season in which they are transforming materials. If they are forced away from a transformation in progress, refer to the rules under "Distractions from Studies" in ArM4, page 95.

At the end of the season, assuming that the natural magician's Lab total of Intelligence + Alchemy + Philosophiae + aura + alchemical bonuses is at least 15, the material is successfully enchanted. For every 5 full points over 15, an additional piece is produced. It is possible to improve this process through magical experimentation (see ArM4, page 92).

Medicine

Natural magicians can use alchemy to enhance their healing ability. With access to a laboratory, a natural magician can produce medicines which allow them to add their Alchemy score (including the +4 bonus to healing and health) to all Medicine rolls they make. Producing such medicines generally takes several hours.

Longevity Potions

Natural magicians can create longevity potions for themselves. Longevity potions produced with natural magic work the same way Hermetic longevity potions do, save that the Lab total used is Intelligence + Alchemy + 3 (the alchemical bonus for healing and health) + Philosophiae + aura. If the natural magician brews the potion for his own benefit, the bonus to aging rolls is –1 for every 5 points of Lab total in the potion. If created for another, it is –1 for every 10 points of Lab total. As with Hermetic longevity potions, additional vis above that which is needed to create the potion gives +1 to the Lab total per pawn of vis used.

Spellcrafting

Even as natural magicians excel at alchemy and astrology, they can also craft spells. To craft a spell the natural magician must assemble appropriate materials, then arrange and prepare them in a particular fashion. The heart of a dove wrapped in red silk and tied with a bit of black thread would be a typical example of such an assemblage.

To craft a spell a natural magician must first determine the level of the desired effect. For this purpose, natural magic functions just like Hermetic magic. See ArM4, page 103 for information on how to determine effect levels. Spells crafted by natural magicians are bound by the limits of Hermetic magic, as described in ArM4, page 67.

Once the effect level is known, the natural magician must try to successfully cast it. To do this, the natural magician must equal or exceed the level of effect on a stress die + Intelligence + Alchemy + Philosophiae + aura + any applicable Form and Effect bonuses + any bonuses for having appropriate spell foci. The only restriction is that the total of bonuses gained from Form and Effect bonuses and spell foci bonuses cannot be greater than the natural magician's Intelligence + Philosophiae, which represents how well the natural magician knows how to use natural materials in casting spells. If a single material is listed as having both a Form and Effect bonus and a bonus as a spell focus, use only the greater of these two values (see the Form and Effect Bonus Table in ArM4, page 84).

Vis can also be spent to increase the spellcasting total. For every extra pawn of vis used in this way the casting roll is increased by five, to a maximum bonus of the natural magician's Intelligence + Alchemy + Philosophiae. Decisions regarding this sort of vis expenditure must be made before the casting die is rolled. Natural magicians must use vis that is attuned to one of the Arts that is tied to the effect.

When casting the spell, the natural magician must spend 15 minutes in uninterrupted work for every 5 levels of the spell. At the end of this time the die is rolled, and if the result equals or exceeds the level of the spell, it is successfully cast. The caster loses two fatigue levels regardless of the spell's success or failure.

All spells that Hermetic magi could cast, including spontaneous, formulaic, and ritual spells, may be cast in this way. However, when a natural magician casts a spell which would be considered a ritual spell, he must expend raw vis just as a Hermetic magus must. Similarly, if the Hermetic version of the spell can have its range or duration boosted through the use of vis then the natural magic spell can be extended in the same fashion. This is not the same as using vis to increase the spellcasting total, as described above.

The assemblage of materials must remain together while the spell is in effect. If the assemblage is disturbed or destroyed before the spell ends, the effect is immediately canceled. Assemblages for spells cast on a specific target must remain near the target for the duration of the effect. Such assemblages are commonly carried or worn by their recipient.

All of the components used in crafting a spell are reusable in subsequent spells, with the exception of any vis used and any components that are burned, consumed, or otherwise used up.

Enchantments

Natural magicians can create enchanted items, but within some very specific guidelines. First, they must be created using the rules for lesser enchanted devices (see ArM4, page 88). Second, they must have the effect frequency "constant use." (see ArM4, page 86). In effect, the natural magician is enchanting an assemblage so that it remains permanently magical. Such an assemblage may be built into other items such as wands, staves, weapons, and clothing.

To create an enchanted assemblage the Lab total is Intelligence + Philosophiae + Alchemy + any Form and Effect bonuses + aura. As with Hermetic magi, the Lab total must equal or exceed

Example Spellcrafting

Roger is sailing from Venice to Sicily when a storm arises. He worries that as the storm's intensity increases it may endanger the ship. Roger decides to craft a spell to calm the waves around the ship. He retires to his cabin and prepares.

He wants to control, in a natural fashion, an amount of liquid which is part of a larger body. This is a ReAq effect with a base level of 10. He would like the effect to take place at Near range (within about 15 paces of him), as long as he concentrates, and he would like it to affect the ship (a Structure). The final level of the effect is 25.

Roger spends an hour and fifteen minutes arranging the crystal and other materials in his cabin. At the end of that time, he rolls a 7. The total is 7 (his roll) + 3 (his Intelligence) + 6 (his Alchemy score) + 6 (his Philosophiae score) + 3 (for a piece of beryl which gives a +3 bonus to affect water), for a total of 25. He succeeds, just barely.

The waves all subside just before they reach the ship, and will continue to do so as long as Roger concentrates on the spell. The crew praise their marvelous luck and Roger leaves them none the wiser.

Example Enchantment

A minor noble in Paris seeks fame and attention. He goes to Louis, a natural magician, for help. The noble states that price is no object. Louis suggests a small enchanted charm which will make the noble appear more forceful and authoritative. The noble is quite pleased with this idea. Louis says it will be ready in a season, but that the price is 3 truffles, each not less than 2 inches in diameter (worth a total of 3 pawns of Creo vis). The noble blanches a little and agrees.

Louis decides to duplicate the effects of the spell *Aura of Ennobled Presence* (MuIm 10). The final effect level is 10, since the +5 for constant use is not added in.

Louis spends a season in enchantment, and spends 1 pawn of Muto vis. He decides to use an amethyst as the focus of the enchantment, so his Lab total is 3 (his Intelligence) + 6 (his Alchemy score) + 6 (his Philosophiae score) + 5 (for the amethyst), for a total of 20. Since 20 is double the level of effect, Louis succeeds.

At the end of the season the noble returns to collect his enchanted amethyst and gives Louis his truffles.

twice the effect level. Because of the special nature of this type of enchantment, the +5 modifier to the level of the enchantment due to "constant use" is not applied. The enchantment is treated as an ordinary Hermetic enchantment in all other ways, including vis requirements. As with Hermetic magi, natural magicians are limited in the level of effect they can instill. They may never use more vis in an item than they have Philosophiae + Alchemy.

A natural magicians can use additional vis to increase his Lab total. Each pawn of vis so expended grants a +5 bonus. Vis affiliated with any Art may be used for this purpose.

Like Hermetic magi, natural magicians can create enchanted items which protect against magic. Every 5 levels of effect act as 5 levels of magic resistance.

Natural Magicians Summary of Formulae

Brew Potions
Lab total = Intelligence + Alchemy + Alchemy bonuses + Philosophiae + aura

Transformation
Lab total = Intelligence + Alchemy + Alchemy bonuses + Philosophiae + aura; ease factor is 15+; for every 5 full points over 15, an additional piece is produced.

Longevity Potion
Lab total = Intelligence + Alchemy + 3 + Philosophiae + aura + (1 x pawns of vis)

Spellcrafting
stress die + Intelligence + Alchemy + Philosophiae + aura + Form and Effect bonuses + spell foci bonuses; ease factor is level of effect.

Maximum Spellcrafting Form and Effect bonuses
Intelligence + Philosophiae

Maximum Spellcrafting Bonus from Vis
Intelligence + Alchemy + Philosophiae

Enchant an Assemblage
Lab total = Intelligence + Philosophiae + Alchemy + Form and Effect bonuses + aura; Lab total must equal or exceed twice the effect level.

Spirit Masters

The spirit masters claim that theirs is the oldest tradition of hedge wizardry in Mythic Europe. Whether their claims are true, it is clear that they have been around for many centuries. However, getting information about the spirit masters is seldom easy since they are also the most secretive of the four groups discussed here.

Spirit masters have one primary ability: they can summon and speak with all manner of magical beings. However, they lack any method of binding

or coercing the beings they summon, so the essence of being a successful spirit master is proficiency in bargaining.

All spirit master mystic companion characters start with the following Abilities at no cost. Spirit masters have a minimum age of 20.

Bargain 3

Charm 2

Legend Lore 3

Magic Sensitivity 2

Occult Lore 4

Second Sight 2

Summoning 4

Summonings

Spirit masters can summon any creature, person, or spirit that has connections beyond the mortal world but is not tied to Heaven, Hell, or Arcadia. This includes:

- Magical creatures (any creature with a Magical Might score)

- Beasts of Virtue (described in Chapter 4)

- Airy spirits (described in Chapter 4)

- Ghosts whose bodies were not given a Christian burial

- Hermetic magi and others who work magic

Spirit masters can also summon mundane people and animals that they have arcane connections to. Since the demons of Hell are masters of deceit, they may choose to answer a spirit master's call. Divine and Faerie powers will not usually allow themselves to be summoned.

Specific individuals can be summoned with as much ease as general representatives of a given type of individual. For instance, it is as easy to summon a specific dragon known by name as it is to summon any old dragon. Alternatively, a spirit master may specify a specific subset of a type of creature. For example, a spirit master could specify a white rabbit, or a Halcyon with a Might of 25.

This ability to summon a vast array of magical beings is quite powerful, but there are several limitations on summoning. First, spirit masters cannot bind or control beings once they have been summoned—they must rely on their bargaining skills to arrive at an agreement. Second, summoned beings do not appear before the spirit master. They arrive to bargain in a natural fashion from the nearest available location. For instance, a spirit of Cholera will remove itself from the nearest Cholera victim and travel to the summoner. Third, a spirit master cannot determine the exact moment or location the spirit will approach, and if the spirit master leaves the general area where he performed the summoning ritual, the being summoned is released from its obligation. Finally, when a spirit and spirit master are finished bargaining, the spirit returns to its original location unless a bargain has been struck.

Spirit masters do possess four traits which help them deal effectively with the beings which they summon. First, spirit masters can communicate with any being they summon. Second, spirit masters are able to see spirits and sense magic, using the Exceptional Abilities Second Sight and Magic Sensitivity. Third, they gain a +3 bonus to their Presence and Communication Characteristics when dealing with summoned beings. Finally, spir-

Ex Miscellanea Spirit Masters

Some spirit masters have made a transition to the Order of Hermes and have been trained in Hermetic Magic. In fact, members of this group of Ex Miscellanea magi are presented in ArM4, page 23. Now that these rules are available, you can create characters that run the gamut from mystic companion spirit masters who have been integrated into the Order but have no other Hermetic powers to characters created using the rules for Hermetic magi but have some of the Virtues listed on page 55, like Summoner and Magical Ally.

it masters can create circles which may protect them from dangerous spirits.

Summoning Procedure

Summoning a spirit takes preparation; the spirit master must purify the site, create any necessary preconditions (such as a fire for a Salamandrus), and, if desired, draw a protective circle. These preparations take approximately one full hour.

The protective circle is for the spirit master and any clients or assistants to stand within. In a pinch, a protective circle can be drawn in two rounds. The strength of the circle is a stress die + Intelligence + Occult Lore (or Legend Lore when summoning a magical beast) + Summoning + Concentration + aura. Spirits and magical beings with a Might score equal to or less than this total are unable to enter the circle or harm those within it. If two circles are drawn, the second circle dispels the first. A protective circle may be made anywhere from 3 to 7 paces across. It remains active until the spirit master leaves it. When the spirit arrives it is always outside of this circle.

In order to successfully summon a being the spirit master must equal or exceed the ease factor listed on the Summoning Ease Factor table using a stress die + Presence (include the spirit master's +3 bonus) + Summoning + Occult Lore (or Legend Lore) + Charm + aura. Every attempted summoning costs the summoner two fatigue levels.

There are some barriers to successful summoning based on the ability of the being summoned to go to the spirit master. Magical creatures and airy spirits will generally be able to travel to any location in the mundane world with little difficulty, as they are accustomed to traveling in the Realm of Magic. They can be summoned with great reliability. Beasts of Virtue will respond unless they are physically restrained (for example, they are caged or injured). Hermetic magi and other magic users feel compelled to respond to summons, and must make an effort to reach the spirit master. They may not realize that they are being compelled, and

may instead find other rationalizations for their travels. If they are capable, magic users may opt to communicate magically with the spirit master to fulfill the obligation of their summoning. People who are summoned over great distances may arrive in a cranky frame of mind if they were busy with important things elsewhere. They may demand recompense from the spirit master simply for the inconvenience of travel. Spirit masters should be mindful of this, though it does not hinder their abilities in any way other than making their bargaining more difficult.

Thinking beings are not under a mind-numbing compulsion to go to the site of the summoning. If a spirit master successfully summons a Hermetic magus, for example, the magus feels an intense desire to journey to the site of the summoning. This desire can be ignored if there is an immediate, pressing need to do something else.

Summoned beings that cannot answer the call because they are restrained, injured, or compelled by some other force continue to feel compelled by the summoning, but remain bound by whatever force is keeping them away. The compulsion ends when the spirit master gives up on the summoning.

In no case can a spirit master successfully summon a being that is already responding to the call of another spirit master.

Summonings do not require vis. If the summoner has the name of or an arcane connection to the subject of the summoning, a specific magical being may be summoned. Otherwise, some representative of the desired type of creature will be summoned.

If summoned successfully, the being usually arrives curious and in a neutral or positive frame of mind. If the summoning botches, something undesirable may arrive, or the being may show up feeling quite hostile.

When corporeal beings like magi or magical animals are summoned they must journey to the site by means at their command, which may take longer than the journey of a summoned airy spirit. It is important to note that a summoning calls the summoned being to the site where the summoning took place. If the spirit master leaves that area, the compulsion ends.

Bargaining

Spirit masters must bargain with the beings they summon. Some ghosts may help their descendants for free, while other spirits demand a heavy price to perform any action. Unless there is some preexisting problem, most spirits are inclined to like and respect spirit masters; most spirits will deal fairly with their summoners. This does not mean that spirits will not demand a fair price for their services.

Spirits and beast of virtue are magical beings and are bound by their word. Such beings always uphold their end of a bargain if the spirit master does the same. Living magi and other mundane humans who are summoned may break their word, but angry spirit masters can be potent foes. Some spirit masters are noted for their skill at making tricky and deceptive bargains. Demons who come impersonating airy spirits are bound by their word, but are often remarkably clever and literal when interpreting the promises they give.

Exactly what a summoned being will ask for varies wildly. Magi often want vis or information. Ghosts may want anything from a proper burial to aid for their descendants. Beasts of virtue may

desire better homes or aid against foes. Airy spirits might bargain for anything from vis, to bonfires lit in their honor, to odd vows from the summoner, such as never damming a river. The exact nature of the price depends both on the nature of the summoned being and the bargaining skill of the summoner.

Spirit masters may use threats instead of promises as bargaining tools, but such spirit masters had best be exceedingly careful in the wording of their bargains. There a number of stories of such spirit masters coming to bad ends.

It is important to note that all bargains must be agreed upon by both the summoner and the summoned being before the summoned being will take any action for the summoner. Payment may be demanded in advance or deferred until a specific later time.

While spirit masters cannot create charms or potions of longevity like cunning-folk or natural magicians, they can use their ability to bargain to cheat the specter of old age, bargaining with certain airy spirits for longer lives. As a result of each

Example Summoning

Laura is the only daughter of an impoverished noble family. She has heard a legend that Charles, her great, great, grandfather amassed a huge treasure fighting the Saracens. This legend has it that Charles was lost at sea, but that before he left he hid the treasure to keep it safe until he returned. No one has seen the treasure since. Laura approaches William, a spirit master, for help.

William asks if Laura has anything which belonged to Charles. Laura gives him a large jeweled ring. William says he may be able to help her. He asks for a tenth of the treasure if it is found, and the ring if the treasure is not found. Laura agrees, and William gets to work.

William first spends an hour drawing a protective circle and making other preparations. William's circle score is 3 (his Intelligence) + 5 (his Summoning score) + 5 (his Occult Lore score) + 4 (his Concentration score), for a total of 17. A stress die is rolled secretly, and the roll is 5. The total, then, is 22. If there is trouble the circle will not protect against Charles' ghost, because he is a fairly powerful ghost and has a Spirit Might of 25.

When he is done preparing, William makes his summoning roll of 7. His total is 7 (his roll) + 6 (his Presence + 3) + 5 (his Summoning score) + 5 (his Occult Lore score) + 4 (his Charm score), for a total of 27. He handily summons Charles' ghost.

When it arrives, William negotiates with the ghost. Upon hearing of the poverty of his descendants, Charles is quite happy to reveal the location of the treasure. He only asks that a small chapel to be built in his name with part of the treasure.

William warns Laura that failing to build the chapel will likely have terrible consequences, as will failing to pay William.

such bargain the spirit master receives a span of years in which he does not age, and no aging rolls are made. Bargains that offset aging are without exception very expensive.

In general, a spirit is capable of giving a spirit master a maximum of (Might − 20) years free of aging. However, as time passes, more and more powerful spirits are required. Say a spirit of Might 30 gives a spirit master ten years free of aging. When those ten years are up, the spirit master must contact a spirit of a Might greater than 30, who can only grant the difference between its maximum award and the number of years already awarded. So if the spirit master from the previous example contacted a spirit with a Might of 40, it would only be able to award another ten years.

Allies

All spirit masters gain a magical ally as part of their training; to be accepted as a spirit master, an apprentice must seek out a magical creature and convince it to become his permanent ally. The bond between spirit master and ally is much like the bond between magi and their familiars.

A spirit master and his ally can each sense the other's position and basic state of being. Furthermore, the spirit master can call to the ally to come at any time, without performing a summoning. Both these abilities work regardless of the distance between the two. However, like Hermetic familiars, allies are intelligent, free-willed entities. The bond between spirit master and ally is one of friendship and trust. This relationship can sometimes be the only relationship free from trickery and deception in a spirit master's life. Spirit masters who mistreat their allies will find themselves deserted or betrayed.

There are four basic types of allies, though a few spirit masters seek more exotic allies. The four are ghosts, shadows, airy spirits, and beasts of virtue. Regardless of type, all allies have a Spirit or Magical Might of 20. Whenever the ally is in physical contact with the spirit master, both are protected by the ally's Magic Resistance of 20.

Ghosts

Having a ghost ally is much like having the +4 Virtue Ghostly Warder (ArM4, page 46). The major difference is that the ghost need not be anyone the spirit master knew in life. In addition, these ghosts are not limited in how long they can leave the spirit master's presence. Like Ghostly Warders, ghost allies have 20 experience points in various Abilities. A spirit master who makes an ally of a ghost may see and speak with the ghost when it is nearby, and call it when it is not, but may not otherwise communicate with the ghost when it is far away.

Shadows

Some spirit masters ally themselves with their own shadows. When this is done, the shadow becomes a separable, free-willed, intelligent entity who can be sent away from the spirit master to seek or convey information. Spirit masters can see through their shadow's senses (which are identical to their own senses) and can communicate with the shadow fully regardless of distance. In addition, while shadows cannot manipulate the physical world in any way, they can speak.

Shadows move like ordinary shadows. They can slide under doors, but cannot walk through walls. They can run, but only as fast as their spirit master. Shadows can easily cross water and climb sheer walls. Shadows can also call the spirits of people who are sleeping and either speak with them where they are, or ask them to come to the spirit master. To do this, the spirit master's shadow must touch the sleeping person.

Airy Spirits

Some spirit masters ally themselves with airy spirits—any of the airy spirits listed in Chapter 4 are possibilities excepting Lucifugus and Amphisbenae. Those two types will never ally themselves with any mortal. Allied airy spirits may freely use any of their powers for their spirit master, but may expect favors in return. A spirit master who makes an ally of an airy spirit may see and speak with the spirit when it is nearby, and call it when it is not, but may not otherwise communicate with the spirit when it is far away.

Beasts of Virtue

Beasts of virtue are common ally choices. A beast of virtue ally functions in many ways like a Hermetic familiar. It is fully intelligent and capable of speech. Sometimes such allies are used to convey messages, but it can be difficult to find people who are willing to listen to talking animals. The spirit master and the ally each have a general sense of where the other is and can call to each other when desired.

Spirit Masters Summary of Formulae

Protective Circle Strength
stress die + Intelligence + Occult Lore (or Legend Lore if magical beast) + Summoning + Concentration + aura; being's Might must exceed strength to enter circle.

Summoning
stress die + Presence (include the spirit master's +3 bonus) + Summoning + Occult Lore (or Legend Lore if magical beast) + Charm + aura

Ascetics

Ascetics are the most mysterious and misunderstood of the four types of hedge wizards presented here. Ascetics seek spiritual perfection both through magical practices and by distancing themselves from the mundane world. In doing so, they eschew all facets of mundane life including organized hierarchies like those of the Church and written knowledge including the Bible.

Ascetics seek to transcend the limits of the mortal world and the limits of their mundane bodies through ritual purification and rigorous magical practice. Ascetics see the mortal world as flawed, serving to distract their spirits from the true perfection which can be found when one looks beyond the mortal world to the ethereal realms beyond.

Ascetics can be found throughout Mythic Europe. The Cathars of Southern France have some among their numbers, as do many other heretical groups. Some of the remaining Gnostics in Byzantium are ascetics. Ascetics can also be found among the holy hermits and anchorites who populate Mythic Europe.

Many see ascetics as religious figures, a fact which has brought a number of them into conflict with the Church, because many in the Church believe they are heretics or diabolists. In fact, their practices are much more magical than religious.

Being an ascetic is very different from having True Faith. True Faith involves having faith in God's plan for your life and for the world as a whole. Ascetics have faith in themselves. Most believe in God, but choose to seek God through their mystical practices, rather than asking for God's assistance.

Because of their distance from the mortal world and their connection to powers which transcend the mortal world, the magic of ascetics does not respond normally to auras. When using abilities which are entitled to an aura bonus, ascetics receive a bonus equal to the strength of the aura for magic, divine, and faerie auras. All three are removed from the mortal world, and so help ascetics in their quest to transcend it. Infernal auras give penalties to such activities equal to the strength of the aura. While Infernal auras are also removed from the mortal world, they, by their very nature, are connected to worldly temptation. This temptation distracts ascetics from their quest to renounce the mundane world.

Through their renouncement of the mundane world ascetics gain the ability to transcend some of the limits of their mortal bodies. However, this ability also limits their ability to interact in the mundane world. Ascetics must avoid indulgence of any kind. Suffering and privation are regarded as being just as indulgent as living in extravagant luxury.

Their food must be simple, bland, and not excessive in quantity. Ascetics should not have more possessions than they can easily carry, including dwellings and beasts of burden. Ascetics almost never have sex, and if they do, it is never to procreate. Having children is seen as an act

which connects you firmly to the mortal world and is anathema to ascetics. Most ascetics are either celibate or homosexual. Ascetics must keep clean and avoid disease. They must also wear clothes which are plain and unadorned. Finally, ascetics must avoid engaging in commerce.

Note that these limits are personal prohibitions for ascetics. Most ascetics have no problem with others engaging in these activities, as long as no one attempts to force the ascetic to engage in them too.

Ascetics do not choose a Companion Social Class Virtue. They gain the +1 Companion Social Class Virtue Wise One (ArM4, page 38) at no cost.

Ascetic mystic companion characters start with the following abilities at no cost. Ascetics have no minimum age.

Charm 3

Concentration 5

Leadership 4

Sense Holiness & Unholiness 4

Purity

The storyguide should take note of each ascetic character's behavior and rate his compliance with the ideals of asceticism as described above on a scale between 0 and 5. A score of 0 indicates frequent lapses of a significant nature, and a score of 5 indicates minor lapses occurring quite rarely. A score of 6 is theoretically possible, but would indicate no lapses in behavior. This number is the ascetic's Purity score. Example descriptions are provided in the table below.

An ascetic's Purity score is always based on storyguide (or troupe) evaluation of the ascetic's adherence to asceticism. Ascetics do not gain experience points in Purity, nor can they increase their score by any method other than adhering to the highest ideals of their faith. Given that, however, it is not recommended that an ascetic's Purity be adjusted by more than one point in either direction per session of play, and it is likely that most sessions will not lead to any change in Purity.

Player character ascetics begin play with a Purity score of two, unless the player chooses a lower number to reflect a character who struggles less successfully with his ideals.

An ascetic may add his Purity to all Soak rolls and totals and to all Stamina rolls against poison. He may add his Purity score to all rolls involving Alertness, Concentration, Disputatio, Leadership, Survival, Dowsing, Second Sight, Faerie Sight, Sense Holiness & Unholiness, and Magic Sensitivity as long as he has a score of at least 1 in the Ability in question. Purity can be added to Natural Resistance rolls against magic if desired.

Purity Table

Score	Description
0	Character lapses from the ideals of asceticism constantly.
1	Character has major lapses in behavior no more often than once per week, and has minor lapses no more often than once per day.
2	Character has major lapses no more often than once a month, and has minor lapses no more often than once a week.
3	Character has major lapses no more often than once a season, and has minor lapses no more often than once a month.
4	Character has major lapses no more often than once a year, and has minor lapses no more often than once a season.
5	Character never has major lapses, and has minor lapses no more often than once a year.
6	Character never breaks from the ideals of asceticism.

Ascetics with a Purity score of 3 or higher are immune to all diseases. Finally, an ascetic may subtract twice his Purity score from rolls on the Aging Table (see ArM4, page 181).

Purity hinders ascetics in understanding the world around them. Ascetics must subtract their Purity score from all rolls using Charm, Folk Ken, Guile, and all Social Skills except Leadership.

Transcendence

Ascetics may temporarily transcend the limits of their bodies and of the mundane world. Some of these transcendences are instantaneous effects such as traveling from one city to another in the blink of an eye. Others, such as walking on water or resisting the effects of extreme weather, continue for a period of time. These transcendences continue until the ascetic engages in worldly activity such as eating, sleeping, or engaging in commerce, or until the ascetic attempts to transcend the world again for some different purpose.

When transcending the world, ascetics lose one fatigue level every 12 hours until they eat or sleep. They can avoid this fatigue loss by making a stress roll + Stamina of 12+ each 12 hours. Finally, ascetics can only transcend the mundane world in one fashion at a time (they may become immune to weapons or live without air, for instance, but not both at once).

To transcend the mundane world an ascetic must first decide what he wishes to do. He then spends a time in meditation. At the end of this time he rolls a stress die + Stamina + Concentration + Purity + meditation bonus + aura bonus. The total is compared to a target number for the desired transcendence, which can be found on the Transcendence Table, below. The meditation bonus is determined based on the amount of time the ascetic spent in meditation prior to attempting the transcendence; consult the Meditation Table below for the modifier. Ascetics with the Virtue Strong Will gain +3 to their transcendence total. If the total is greater than or equal to the desired transcendence then the ascetic succeeds. Otherwise he fails. If the roll

Meditation Table

Length of Meditation	Modifier
24 hours	+2
6 hours	+1
1 hour	.0
10 minutes	–3
2 minutes	–6
1 round	–9
no meditation	–12

botches, some undesired transcendence may occur (for example, an ascetic who wanted to be immune to fire might end up in another city).

Other effects than those listed on the Transcendence Table are possible, subject to the following limits.

All magical effects ascetics are capable of producing involve ignoring the limitations of the mortal world (which includes magical effects that occur in the mundane world). They cannot, for instance, start a fire, cause themselves to fall sick, or improve their physical statistics.

Ascetics can only effect themselves with transcendences. An ascetic might be able to walk through a wall, but no one else could go with him. Ascetics who are transported to another place through transcendence may only carry light garments and a few simple possessions along.

Finally, an ascetic trying to perceive or journey to a distant location or person must either be quite familiar with their target or possess an arcane connection to it.

It is said that some ascetics sit down, meditate, and transcend the mundane world forever. This could only happen to the purest of ascetics. If accomplished, the ascetic would never be seen again.

Transcendence Table

12+ Walk on water. Ignore extreme weather. Ignore the weight of a single large object. See in the dark.

15+ Heal one body level. Exist without food, drink, or air.

18+ Walk through a wall. Walk through a bonfire without harm. Take no damage from weapons. Be immune to the direct effects of one Hermetic Form (or a roughly equivalent category of magic from a non-Hermetic tradition).

21+ Observe any single place or person you know (or have an arcane connection to) from any distance. Be immune to the direct effects of one Hermetic Technique (or a roughly equivalent category of magic from a non-Hermetic tradition).

24+ Speak a single message to anyone you know (or have an arcane connection to) and receive a reply, from any distance. Be immune to all magic. Take no damage from any mundane source.

27+ Journey to any place you know (or have an arcane connection to) in the blink of an eye. Be immune to all forms of damage.

Example Transcendence

Paul is an ascetic who is outspoken in his feelings about the injustice of the strong oppressing the weak. In a village near Paul's hut, the lord, Count Dumain, has raised taxes to pay the expense of his planned journey to the Levant. If the peasants are not able to pay they are whipped and driven off their land.

Paul sees the hypocrisy of funding a journey to the Holy Land through the suffering of others and wishes to publicly tell Count Dumain at the feast the Count is holding for the bishop who is about to bless his journey. Paul is well aware that the Count's guards will try to stop him, and that they may try to harm him. Paul decides his point could best be made if he is immune to harm.

On the eve of the feast Paul begins his meditation. He meditates for one hour (for no modifier), and rolls a 6. Paul's transcendence total is 6 (his roll) + 2 (his Stamina) + 6 (his Concentration score) + 3 (his Purity) + 2 (a local Faerie aura), for a total of 19. Immunity to weapons requires a roll of 18+.

Until Paul eats or sleeps he can safely ignore the swords and spears of the Count's guards.

Mystic Understanding

Ascetics know things others do not; this mystic understanding is the most mysterious of their powers. Some clergy say that demons tell them these things. Many peasants say that angels talk to ascetics. Criamon magi say ascetics have found another path to the heart of the Enigma. The actual source remains unclear.

This ability is not the power to learn secrets or hidden facts, but instead the ability to understand the plan of the world in ways others can not.

To use mystic understanding an ascetic must meditate. When an ascetic uses mystic understanding, the player asks the storyguide a short question. The character then meditates for a few moments and rolls a stress die + Purity. On a 9+, it succeeds and some understanding is gained. The storyguide provides a short correct answer to the question. Such answers should generally be one sentence or less. They may reveal a different part of the truth than the character had in mind, but they should be relevant to the subject and ultimately be useful. On a failure nothing is gained, and on a botch the ascetic receives incomprehensible, useless, or incorrect information.

Only a limited amount of understanding can be gleaned about any single topic. An ascetic can

Ascetics
Summary of Formulae

Transcendence
stress die + Stamina + Concentration + Purity + meditation bonus + aura

Mystic Understanding
stress die + Purity; ease factor is 9+

Example Mystic Understanding

Sibylle the ascetic lives at court in Sicily. The Moors of Sicily have been growing increasingly resentful of their Christian rulers. Frederick II, king of Sicily, is at his wits' end to figure out the cause of the sudden rise in strife. When all other options fail, Frederick climbs the long staircase to Sibylle's secluded tower. He asks Sibylle if she has any idea why the Moors are becoming violent. Sibylle agrees to help him. She asks him to come back in the evening.

Sibylle kneels on the floor and meditates on this question. She rolls a 7. Her total is 7 (her roll) + 4 (her Purity), for a total of 11. This exceeds the ease factor of 9, so she is successful.

When Frederick returns she tells him, "Ask Ali ibn Musa." Frederick knows Ali ibn Musa to be one of the most prominent Moors in Palermo and finds this fine advice.

However, what neither he nor Sibylle knows is that the reason the Moors are upset is that Ali ibn Musa has been collecting fictitious taxes in Frederick's name. These taxes serve to enrich Ali while also hopefully inciting the Moors to riot. Ali then plans to act as the Moors representative, claim he has gotten the fictitious taxes repealed and enjoy both his ill-gotten wealth, and the power he has gained from becoming the Moors' official representative.

ask no more than three questions on any single topic.

This ability can prove difficult for inexperienced storyguides. Players should not be allowed to use mystic understanding to circumvent obstacles if the storyguide does not wish to allow it, or when it abbreviates interesting stories. When in doubt, storyguides should err on the side of less information. The insights of mystic understanding can be as cryptic as the questions themselves.

New Virtues

The Virtues and Flaws listed below allow characters who are not mystic companions the chance to gains some of the characteristics of hedge wizards. These Virtues and Flaws are open to any companion. At the troupe's option, magi and grogs may also be allowed to select these Virtues and Flaws.

Folk Magician (+2): This Virtue gives you the Exceptional Knowledge Folk Magic at a score of 1. You can increase your score by spending experience points, just as you can with other Abilities. This Virtue also allows you to recognize and use wild vis as cunning-folk do.

Greater Herbalism (+2): In addition to gaining all the benefits of the +1 Virtue Herbalism (see ArM4, page 41), you are able to create potions and minor potions like those created by cunning-folk (see pages 34-36).

Charm Maker (+2): You are able to make lesser and greater charms just like those made by cunning-folk, following the standard rules that begin on page 37. By purchasing this Virtue, you gain the Exceptional Skill Craft Charm with an initial score of 1 . You may spend experience points to increase your score, as with other Abilities.

Bane Maker (+2): You are able to make lesser and greater banes just like those made by cunning-folk, following the standard rules that begin on page 37. By purchasing this Virtue, you gain the Exceptional Skill Craft Bane with an initial score of 1 . You may spend experience points to increase your score, as with other Abilities.

Guild Alchemist (+4): In the early thirteenth century, in the large cities of Mythic Europe, guilds are forming. One such guild is the Guild of Alchemists and Apothecaries. These alchemists sell their wares in cities and at traveling fairs. Guild training assures that members have a minimum level of competence before they are allowed to practice. However, members must pay guild dues, abide by the guild rules of secrecy, and accept the guild's rulings about prices. You are a member of the Guild of Alchemists and Apothecaries, and have a minimum age of (22 – Intelligence).

All guild alchemists begin with 3 levels in the Exceptional Ability Alchemy (but need not take the +1 Virtue Alchemy), 3 Levels in Philosophiae, 3 levels in Speak Latin and 3 levels in Scribe Latin. Guild alchemists can create potions and bring about transformations as natural magicians do (see pages 41-42).

This Virtue may be selected by a companion as a Companion Social Class Virtue, or may be selected as a regular Virtue.

Magical Ally (+4): You had partial training as a spirit master, during which time you found a magical ally and bargained with it for its companionship. Use the guidelines found on pages 48-49 for selecting your ally. These rules also govern the way your ally behaves in play.

Mystic Understanding (+4): You can achieve mystic understanding just like an ascetic can (see pages 53-54). If you have no Purity score, use the average of your Intelligence and Perception, rounded up, in the place of Purity for purposes of mystic understanding.

Natural Enchantment (+4): You have been trained in the construction of enchantments using the disciplines of natural magic. You use the same rules that natural magicians do to construct enchanted devices (see pages 43-44). Characters with this Virtue may purchase the Ability Philosophiae (which is normally only available to educated characters), but gain no initial score in it.

Natural Spellcrafting (+5): Your education and background allow you to craft and cast spells using the same rules that natural magicians use (see pages 42-43). Characters with this Virtue may purchase the Ability Philosophiae (which is normally only available to educated characters), but gain no initial score in it.

Summoner (+5): You are able to summon creatures, people, and spirits just as spirit masters do (see page 44-48). You know how to draw a protective circle, and gain the Exceptional Talent Summoning. You have a score of 1 in Summoning, but may spend experience points to increase your score just as you can with other Abilities.

Purity (+6): You strive to live according to the ideals of asceticism, and due to this striving, you have a Purity score. This score functions just like Purity does for ascetics (see pages 51-52). You may also attempt transcendences as ascetics do.

New Abilities

All of the new Abilities listed in this section are Exceptional Abilities. There are only two ways that a character can learn them. The first is for the character to be a member of a tradition of hedge wizardry that grants one or more of these Abilities to starting members of that tradition. For example, all cunning-folk mystic companions begin with the Abilities Craft Charm, Craft Bane, and Folk Magic. The second way is for a character to purchase a Virtue that specifically allows the character to spend experience on them. For example, the new Virtue Folk Magician stipulates that the character gains the Ability Folk Magic.

Exceptional Talents

Summoning: This Ability allows characters to summon creatures, people, and beasts in the manner described for spirit masters on pages 44-48. This ability does allow the summoner to communicate with any being summoned, but does not confer any special ability to see beings that are otherwise obscured. The Exceptional Abilities Second Sight and Magic Sensitivity are required for that. *Specialties: beasts of virtue, ghosts, magi, elemental spirits, spirits of artifice, spirits of sickness.* (Intelligence)

Faerie Sight: Faerie Sight is similar to the Exceptional Ability Second Sight (see ArM4, page 42), but this version allows characters to perceive faerie things rather than things associated with the Realm of Magic. It also allows characters to see through faerie illusions on a Faerie Sight stress roll of 12+. Finally, it allows characters to see into faerie regiones as described in ArM4 on page 245. *Specialties: regiones, faerie illusions, faerie beings.* (Perception)

Exceptional Skills

Craft Charm: Characters with this Ability can craft charms according to the standard rules for doing so, found on page 37. *Specialties: health, fortune, wealth, endurance.* (Intelligence)

Craft Bane: Characters with this Ability can craft banes according to the standard rules for doing so, found on page 37. *Specialties: disease, misfortune, insanity, emotions.* (Intelligence)

Exceptional Knowledges

Folk Magic: This Ability confers knowledge of the practices of folk magic. You know what sorts of natural items are good for which sorts of magical applications, and can use that knowledge to assist you in your work. In game terms, Folk Magic provides a bonus to most of the magical endeavors cunning-folk undertake. *Specialties: charms, banes, potions.* (Intelligence)

Other Traditions

The four types of hedge wizards listed here are the four most common varieties found in Mythic Europe, but other traditions also exist. The information in this section provides guidelines for creating your own hedge wizards.

When creating your own hedge wizard traditions it is important to think of some thematic concept that describes the tradition's scope and breadth. Old stories and legends can provide a wealth of ideas about medieval hedge magic. The problem with such legends is that they can be remarkably vague in describing exactly what a given wizard can do. This is why a thematic concept is useful—otherwise it is easy to come up with a tradition which consists of a grab bag of unrelated powers. Such wizards are neither interesting nor appropriate to the setting.

Powers

When creating new types of mystic companions it is important to keep their power level in mind. Mystic companions should be significantly more powerful than ordinary companions, but less powerful than Hermetic magi. Members of the Order of Hermes are supposed to be the most powerful magi in Mythic Europe.

Mystic companions from the traditions in this book each have special powers and abilities equal to about ten points of free Virtues. For example, natural magicians all possess abilities similar to the Virtues Alchemy (+1), Magister in Artibus (+3), and Magic Sensitivity (+1). They also have the Ability to cast spells using lengthy rituals (given a value of +5 in the "New Virtues" section, above). There is no science involved in the number ten, however. As long as you get storyguide approval, you can fudge by a few points on either side of ten. The most important thing is that the tradition make sense as a collection of powers and abilities, and that it fit the saga.

When actually creating powers, it is always easier to use existing material than to create your own. The charms and banes of cunning-folk are similar to the Gruagach Virtues Curse and Gift (see *Lion of the North*), for example. Similarly, natural magicians work magic which is somewhat similar to (if much more limited than) Hermetic Magic. Hermetic spell levels are used as a way of rating the power of natural magicians.

These types of modifications lead to characters who are different in play, but who use mechanics that mesh with the rest of the game. It is certainly possible to create totally new magic systems for hedge wizards, but care must be taken to make sure these magic systems are not unbalancing in play.

Abilities

Like Hermetic magi, fully trained mystic companions go through an apprenticeship where they are trained in Abilities. During their apprenticeships, Hermetic magi accumulate 45 experience points in a variety of abilities such as Speak Latin and Magic Theory. Each of the four types of hedge wizard listed here has 41 experience points worth of Abilities (in addition to Speak Own Language at a score of 5), and each receives (age +10) experience points more. Your traditions should also give 41 points worth of Abilities, and allow (age + 10) discretionary points.

Chapter 4
Book of Secrets

During my stay with Gerard the Cunning-man I helped him gather magical herbs for his potions and charms. He told me of the virtues of many plants, and created a charm for good luck which I wear to this day. When my time with Gerard was finished and I resumed my rounds, I carried samples of these plants to Mistridge, as it was my first stop. The Magi of Mistridge listened to my tale with interest and then examined several of the plants I brought them. The bit of papaver I brought them contained vis, but the other samples did not. I am sure all these plants were what Gerard referred to as plants of virtue, and yet one contains vis and the others do not. There seem mysteries in this world beyond what is known by our Order.

—From a report on hedge wizards by Passer of Mercere

Natural Marvels

Being a text describing the miraculous virtues of certain herbs and stones, such as are found by the cunning folk and created by the works of natural magic. Also being a description of certain miraculous beasts to be found both in distant places and near at hand.

First, let a theory be proposed here: that among all things, whether mineral, vegetable, or animal, are found some individuals in which power dwells. This power has been called vis. In all individuals of some kinds, this power is much stronger, so that, among stones, any adamas found is likely to possess power, while so few pieces of mud-stone carry power that the nature of its power has never been recorded. In the same way, most poppies carry power, while few daisies do. Among animals, beasts such as the unicorn may always carry power, while some dragons may carry less power than others, and a few are no more than great serpents. As is well known, most goats' blood is no hotter than that of horses, for the ones in which power dwells are rare.

The stones, herbs, and beasts which possess power are here known as Stones, Herbs, and Beasts of Virtue.

A question naturally arises concerning whether human beings also follow this rule.

Hermetic magi have been heard to say a hircus is to a goat as a magus is to a man, but this speculation favors their pride without explaining the dracones, unicornes, gryphones, and other beasts who seem to carry power in most individuals of their kind. Man may be numbered among these creatures. Our power would then be manifest in the unique gifts of our intelligence and our immortal souls, which are possessed by all.

The theory which has just been given is offered for the convenience of students who find a system in which knowledge can be classified useful. It is not intended to represent the truth, which God alone knows, but to be a useful tool for consideration.

Game statistics for the materials of virtue described in this chapter appear in indented, italicized sections such as this one. First, each materi- *al is described by a rarity, which tells how common the mundane version of the material is. Second, the number of pawns of wild vis and number of pawns of standard vis that are found in a single plant, stone, or beast are also listed. Finally, any special powers of each material are described in game terms. When in doubt, use these rules rather than relying on the flavorful (but often imprecise or slippery) descriptions of each herb.*

Objects of virtue are much rarer than their mundane equivalents. For the most common mundane materials, only around one in a thousand stones, herbs, or animals is an object of virtue. On the other hand, even things that are scarce do not always possess virtue. There are certainly mundane diamonds—that is, those that do not have the properties of an Adamas.

Most materials of virtue produce special effects usable by anyone, whether they can use or detect the vis that courses through them. Game mechanics will be provided where necessary. Items of virtue that produce spell-like effects which are described with specific levels may be resisted by individuals and creatures that have magic resistance.

There are two ways to acquire the materials of virtue listed below. First, cunning-folk have a chance to find them. See the rules for finding wild vis on pages 36-37. Second, natural magicians have the ability to transform normal items into items of virtue. See "Transformations" on pages 41-42.

Stones of Virtue

Adamas (diamond)

This stone is clear white like water, but of such virtue that no thing natural or created may cut it, except for itself and the blood of a Hircus. It gives the virtue of making greater the endurance and resolve of the one who wears it.

Very Rare
Wild Vis: 1
Standard Vis: 0
Anyone who carries an adamas gains the equivalent of the +1 Virtue Enduring Constitution and the +1 Virtue Strong-Willed for as long as he carries the stone.

Amandinus (banded agate)

This stone is of many colors, all in patterns. It gives to the one who carries it great knowledge of things that are hidden.

Uncommon
Wild Vis: 1
Standard Vis: 0
The bearer of this stone gains the Exceptional Talent Magic Sensitivity, with a skill level of 3, for as long as he carries this stone.

Amethystus (amethyst)

This stone is of a wine color, clear and fine. Its virtue ends all confusion in whatever part it touches, so that it has been carried in the mouth for clear speech, upon the head to ward off madness of the moon, and on the belly of one who wishes to keep sound wits while drinking.

Uncommon
Wild Vis: 2
Standard Vis: 1 (Mentem)
Anyone carrying an amethystus in the mouth gains +1 Communication while it is carried. If it is carried or worn on the head it cures all madness, both natural or magical. If worn on the body it keeps the bearer from acting foolish when drunk.

Asbestos (salamander hairs)

This stone is of a most strange softness, being the hairs of the salamander. It takes of the nature of the salamander the following virtue: no fire may consume it, but is consumed instead by it and drawn up within, so that it burns continually, but only upon the stone, and may not be put out. It is said that in a former time there was a magician who had woven of this stone a coat, which shone like the sun, moving like a torch in darkness and not burned by any fire.

Rare
Wild Vis: 2
Standard Vis: 1 (Ignem)
Asbestos acts as a Perdo Ignem spell of level 5; it will put out a small bonfire at a touch. Afterwards, it glows with the light of several torches until such time as this fire would have naturally burned out. This glow produces no heat.

Chalazios (quartz pebble)

This stone appears as a small pebble, pure white and cool to the touch. It is found on mountains, being formed of ice which has not melted for a hundred years. Its coolness is such that it cannot be heated, even in the hottest of fires. By this virtue, no man touching such a stone can be inflamed by the hotter passions, such as lust and anger.

Common
Wild Vis: 1
Standard Vis: 0
Anyone carrying a Chalazios cannot feel anger, lust, or any other violent emotion for as long as he carries the stone

Chalcedonius (dripstone)

This stone is found often in places beneath the earth. It is of a brownish color, sometimes gray, and has the feel of hardened wax. When pierced through and worn about the neck, it gives to the wearer its virtue of not being deceived by lies mundane or magical, no matter how cleverly made. This stone is often seen among those who would see through the illusions of witches and magi, but most often in the law courts.

Common
Wild Vis: 2
Standard Vis: 1 (Imáginem)
Anyone wearing a Chalcedonius can see through a magical illusion on a Perception roll of 3 + (magnitude of the illusion), and can discern truth from falsehood on a Perception roll of 6+ for as long as he wears this stone.

Corralus (precious coral)

This stone grows beneath the sea as an herb, and is transformed into a stone on touching the world above. Its virtue is sovereign over that which flows; so that, touched to a wound, it stanches bleeding, while touched to the sea, it calms the waves.

Rare
Wild Vis: 2
Standard Vis: 1 (Aquam)
If placed on a wound a Corralus acts as the spell Bind Wound (CrCo 10), with Instant duration. If placed in a body of water it acts as the spell Break the Oncoming Wave (ReAq 10).

Draconites (ammon's stone, dragon's stone)

This stone comes only from the heads of wyrms and dragons, as can be clearly seen by its form, which curls about itself as the bodies of such beasts do. The draconites holds a part of the power of dragons. Taken from the dragon dead, its virtue is that no one who wears it tied closely to the body can be overcome by fleshy means, neither by wound or poison, so long as it is kept against the skin.

Taken from the dragon alive, its virtue is so great that one who keeps it close against the skin may not die by any means, so long as it is kept against the skin.

Rare
Wild Vis: 6
Standard Vis: 3 (Corpus)
Anyone who carries a Draconites taken from a dead dragon will never suffer any penalties from wounds or poison. Wounds and poison can kill the bearer of such a stone, but this person cannot be rendered unconscious, and suffers no penalties from wounds up to the moment of death.
Wearing a draconites taken from a living dragon prevents death by any means. The wearer does age and accumulate Decrepitude, but will not die of old age. Similarly, the wearer may still be wounded or poisoned, but will always recover. The wearer of such a stone may be incapacitated, but not killed or maimed. Wearing a Draconites neither speeds nor inhibits natural healing. Both kinds of Draconites are worth 6 pawns of wild vis and 3 pawns of Corpus vis.
It is not possible for a natural magician to create Draconites through a transformation, nor is it possible to transform a Draconites taken from a dead dragon into one taken from a living dragon.

Electorus (capon stone)

This stone is found only within a cock which does not crow. To whatever part it touches it brings satisfaction, so that in our own time it has been found that one who holds it in the mouth will find thirst and hunger eased. By the nature of the stone, any part of the body may be similarly comforted.

Uncommon
Wild Vis: 2
Standard Vis: 1 (Imáginem)

The electorus removes discomfort from the part of the body it touches. Individuals who are dying of thirst and carry an electorus in their mouths will still die of thirst, but will feel no discomfort or incapacitation up to the moment of death. Similarly, if this stone is bound against a wound the stone removes all pain and negative modifiers the wound causes, but does not heal it in any way.

Gerachidem (arsenic)

This stone shines like lead, very softly, and of the gray of falcons' wings. When held in the mouth, its virtue is to make men past all care and trouble, and most pleasing to their enemies. It has also been called Arsenicum, and its virtue has been proved in our time.

Uncommon
Wild Vis: 2
Standard Vis: 1 (Perdo)
This stone is poisonous. Anyone who eats Gerachidem or puts it in his mouth dies.

Hephaestites (fool's gold)

This stone shines like the sun and is very heavy, for it holds the virtue of the sun within it. Its attraction is so great that it will draw the heat from any hot thing into itself, so that seething water into which such a stone is dropped will cease to boil. Such a stone sends forth more of the heat it has gathered the more tightly it is gripped. For this reason it is bound with straw and worn upon the chest of those afflicted with cold sicknesses and much coughing, and struck sharply to start fire.

Common
Wild Vis: 1
Standard Vis: 0
A Hephaestites removes heat from any nonliving object it touches; the object is reduced to room temperature. A Hephaestites gives off heat if squeezed or struck. Such heat is sufficient to start a small fire if the stone is struck with force. Gently squeezing it produces a gentle warmth.

Iris (crystal)

This stone appears as clear as water and without color. In form it is horned, sometimes at either end. It has two virtues. If such a stone is held up to the sun, a rainbow will be seen upon the wall beyond. Should this light be shone tightly upon any thing, it will surely catch fire and be consumed. This has been proven in our time.

Uncommon
Wild Vis: 1
Standard Vis: 0
Sunlight which passes through an Iris acts as a level 5 Creo Ignem spell, burning whatever it first touches with a flame like a torch (+5 damage per round). However, to be effective the iris must be held within two paces of the target. If it is held further than this the light merely forms a rainbow.

Lapis Lazuli (lapis lazuli)

This stone is most fine, of a blue like the sky at lauds. Its virtue is such that the bearing of it cures such sickness as goes and returns again, as melancholia and quartan fevers.

Uncommon
Wild Vis: 1
Standard Vis: 0
Anyone carrying a Lapis Lazuli of virtue is affected by an effect similar to Gentle Touch of the Purified Body (CrCo 15) as the stone is carried. The effect is lost and diseases may return when the stone is no longer carried.

Liparea (brimstone)

This stone is very soft. It has a fine yellow color like good butter, but a smell like infernal things. This stone has two virtues. No creature may remain in hiding in any place where it is put, but must come out to where it is. Also, no one who carries it may be attacked by any beast, wild or tame. And this has been proven in our time.

Common
Wild Vis: 2
Standard Vis: 1 (Rego)
If a Liparea is brought within 10 paces of someone who is hiding, the person who is hiding must make a Stamina roll of 9+ or be forced from hiding. No natural animal will ever attack a creature or person carrying such a stone. Even magic cannot force an animal to attack the bearer of a Liparea.

Magnes (lodestone)

This stone is very heavy, of a dark color. It does not show how precious it is to the eye. Its virtue is the power of attraction; any thing which is good or sound it draws to it, but that which is bad or unsound it pushes away. So the infidels use it to test the quality of iron for blades, and a man may carry it below his belt to test the love of a woman. If she is faithful and true in her love, she will be drawn to the wearer right away, but if unfaithful, she will be pushed from him. In this way all things can be tested or divined, so long as that which is to be tested can be put bodily within the reach of the stone, and what is to be known can be answered as true or false.

Rare
Wild Vis: 2
Standard Vis: 1 (Rego)
This stone can be used in tests relating to the quality of the person or object being tested. For people quality refers questions of morals or health only. A Magnes can be used to determine if a blade is sound, if a ship is seaworthy, or if a husband is faithful. It cannot be used to determine if a blade is stolen, or if a person just told a lie, for example.
To perform any test of quality using a Magnes the stone must be placed within 1 pace of the person or object to be tested, and then the person holding the stone must ask a question relating to the quality of the subject of the test. If the subject is of quality it and the Magnes will be attracted together. If the subject is not of quality it will be repelled from the Magnes, or the Magnes from it.

Onyx (onyx)

This stone is black as midnight, banded sometimes with white, and is most often found in those regions which adjoin the world below. Anyone, upon taking up such a stone, will be seized with sorrow and with terrors, and will speak badly to companions, until such a time as the stone is set aside.

Common
Wild Vis: 2
Standard Vis: 1 (Mentem)
Anyone carrying an Onyx of virtue will act as if under the effect of the spell Pains of the Perpetual Worry (CrMe 20) for as long as the stone is carried.

Opthalmus (opal)

This stone is of diverse colors, and shines forth with such brilliance that all who behold it are made blind to any other thing, so long as it is within their view. It is said that in former times, the emperor Constantine carried such a stone about when he went among the people, so that he would not be recognized. Sometimes a second sort of this stone is found, dull and without color. Though such a stone does not hold the eye, it has the following virtue: any thing made of it is white as milk within the air, but when touched with oil or water, it becomes as clear as water. In our own time this has been proved by the natural magician Scotus, who made of this stone a vessel, in which he went beneath the sea and there saw many wonderful things.

Rare
Wild Vis: 4
Standard Vis: 2 (Imáginem)
As long as this stone is visible, people who see it will not pay attention to the appearance of anyone or anything. For example, people who see this stone will not notice what the people around them look like.

Quirita (hoopoe or plover stone)

This stone is very black in color, and found in the nest of the bird upupa, a black and white bird with a crest upon its head. It has the virtue of causing a sleeper to speak his dreams aloud, when it is touched to him. In this fashion all things a man or woman knows may be learned of them, given time.

Rare
Wild Vis: 1
Standard Vis: 0

When touched to a person's head while he sleeps, a Quirita causes that person to describe any dreams he is having. The dreamer dreams naturally, and the individual holding the stone is not able to influence the dreams by asking questions or using similar means. A Rego Mentem spell of level 15 allows a magi to guide the dreams, however.

Radaim (cockstone)

This stone is found only in the head of a cock, after it has been well cleaned by ants. It has the following virtue. If it be given to anyone, and such a person must take the stone by his own will, he must then give to the one who had the stone whatever thing he next asks for, if it be within the power of the one who has taken the stone to provide that thing.

Uncommon
Wild Vis: 1
Standard Vis: 0

If given to someone who accepts it, a Radiam forces that person to reciprocate with whatever single item is next requested by the giver. If items of exceptional value or worth are requested (storyguide's judgment), the victim may attempt to use magical resistance against a Rego Mentem effect of level 30. If resistance is successful, no gift is required.

If a person is forced to accept a Radiam by means of magic, that person is not affected by the power of the stone.

Selenites (moonstone)

This stone partakes of the nature of the moon, and is found within the head of those creatures which have such a nature, as crabs and toads and turtles, from which it is also known as chelonites. Such a stone has power only at the full of the moon. Its virtue is this; that anyone putting it under the tongue at the full of the moon shall then begin to prophesy, and continue to prophesy until it is removed.

The stone shall decide all that is uncertain which it touches, so that one who knows not which plan to follow shall be decided upon touching it. If the plan is a good one, then it will be set about immediately, but if it is not good, the heart of the one touching such a stone shall shrink from carrying out such a thing.

If touched to one who is in a fever, or any sickness that goes and comes again, the sickness will right away be decided. If the sufferer is to get well, it will occur immediately, and if the sufferer is to die, that will happen right away. In this way the Selenites decides all crises, if it is used at the full of the moon.

Uncommon
Wild Vis: 4
Standard Vis: 2 (Imáginem)
Anyone who places a Selenites under his tongue when a full moon is overhead has visions. Treat this as if the user had the Exceptional Ability Visions (ArM4, page 44) with a score of 5.

Selenites can also help the undecided to make decisions when the moon is full. When an individual has a complicated or important choice to make, and has already spent some time in deliberation, he may touch a Selenites. Upon touching it, the storyguide tells the character which decision he has made (based on the character's personality and motivations as interpreted by the storyguide), and also tells the character whether he feels compelled to immediately implement his decision (based on the storyguide's interpretation of whether the decision is a good one).

If a Selenites is touched to a sick or wounded person at the full moon, the storyguide should determine whether the sickness or wound would eventually be fatal. If not, the person is healed. If so, the person dies.

Topazos (topaz)

This stone is of a clear green or yellow color, very beautiful to the eye. The virtue of this stone is that whatever it touches is calmed right away, and remains calm for as long as the stone touches it. In this way waves have been calmed, or the passions of men and women, or the fury of a wild horse, or the madness of one touched by faeries, or the spells of magi.

Uncommon
Wild Vis: 1

Standard Vis: 0
The touch of this stone calms people and animals, so that they can feel no violent emotion, whether normal or magical, for as long as they touch it. Magical resistance against a Rego Mentem effect of level 30 is allowed. When touched to stormy water it calms the water for a radius of 5 paces around the stone. It may also be used in alchemy to control violent reactions.

Herbs of Virtue

Unless otherwise noted, these herbs of virtue provide their benefits when freshly harvested, until the plant withers. Cunning-folk and characters with Herbalism or Alchemy can preserve these herbs so that their powers extend for years. Even herbs preserved in this way eventually lose their power, though. If required, a simple die divided by two can be used to generate a number of years that a herb will remain effective.

Asphodel (narcissus)

This herb grows at the gates of faerie places, and the ancients said it grew at the borders of the underworld. It has many white flowers together on a stem, like little stars, with a sweet scent. If planted at the door of a place, magic may not be used within that place as long as it is growing, and airy spirits have no power there. Its root cures disease and madness.

Common
Wild Vis: 6
Standard Vis: 3 (Rego)
This plant only protects against magic when it is growing (in the spring and summer). It gives protection equivalent to a level 15 Aegis of the Hearth spell (ReVi Gen), except that everyone is affected by this protection, including the inhabitants of the dwelling. One plant provides protection in a radius of 5 paces or so around it—enough to protect a small hut.

Celandine (celandine)

This plant comes from the earth when the swallows arrive, and withers when they depart. If it is put upon the head of any person, those who are to die soon will begin to sing in a loud voice. Those who will not die soon will weep.

Uncommon
Wild Vis: 2
Standard Vis: 1 (Intéllego)
Like all forms of prophecy this one is vague. Imminent lethal danger and illness which will kill unless treated both cause the subject to sing. However, this does not mean that the predicted death can not be averted.

Chynostates (moonflower)

This herb grows in fields and waste places, and flowers beneath the moon. It partakes of the nature of the moon. Its virtue is that, when ground and anointed on the eyes, the recipient is able to see very clearly and in darkness, his eyes shining out light as do the eyes of beasts that run beneath the moon.

Uncommon
Wild Vis: 1
Standard Vis: 0
An ointment made from this plant functions just like the spell Eyes of the Cat (MuCo 5).

Conium (monk's hood)

This herb has a powerful virtue. If it is given to anyone in food or drink, he will first be seized with great strength, then wild motions like one possessed, and finally with a stillness like death in every way, except that he is aware of his surroundings. If too much of the herb is taken, the person will then die. If not, he will rise and move again with the next rising of the sun. This has been proven by experiment in our own time.

Common
Wild Vis: 2
Standard Vis: 1 (Corpus)
Anyone who ingests this herb gains +3 Strength for several minutes. After that, he loses two short-term fatigue levels, all the while con-

vulsing and raving wildly. After this, he falls into a trance and seems dead, but is still fully aware. This trance lasts for the next full day, after which time he awakens.

Heliotropum (sunflower)

This herb is the herb of the sun. It grows upward toward the sun without ceasing for as long as the summer lasts. Its flowers are like the shape of the sun and turn toward the sun always. Its virtue is such that no one may do evil toward the bearer of the herb, without the bearer dreaming of what has been done and by whom. One who bears it will be seen kindly by strangers.

Common
Wild Vis: 1
Standard Vis: 0
Dreams brought by the heliotropum can either be prophetic, or can occur after the harm has been done. The substance and timing of such dreams are at the discretion of the storyguide. Those who carry this herb receive +1 to Charm rolls.

Jusquiamus (henbane)

The virtue of this herb is poison so strong that nothing can withstand it. It bears a fruit in the form of a pair of jaws, and when these are ground small they will kill any living thing that tastes them, and blacken silver. The herb is sweet to the taste, and pleasing, so that one who bears it in secret, and gives it to no one, is also made pleasing and attractive by it.

Uncommon
Wild Vis: 4
Standard Vis: 2 (Perdo)
Anyone who eats this herb dies. Anyone who carries it secretly gains +1 Presence for the purpose of impressing others for as long as he carries it.

Lilium (lily of the valley)

This herb grows small and pretty in the spring, with flowers like bells. If it is given to anyone, he will cease to sleep, and not sleep until it is put away.

Common
Wild Vis: 1
Standard Vis: 0
No one who carries this herb grows tired, nor needs sleep. Carriers still accrue penalties from fatigue, as normal. However, if this herb is ever removed from a person who has been carrying it, he will immediately fall into a deep sleep lasting one full day for every three days it was carried.

Lingua Canis (hound's tongue)

This herb has a power over dogs, so that if it is put into a place, all the dogs will gather there after a little time, and if it is placed where a dog cannot reach it, the dog will try to reach it until it dies. Any dog that smells this herb will lose its voice and become silent until the sun next rises or sets.

Uncommon
Wild Vis: 1
Standard Vis: 0
Lingua Canis attracts all dogs within a radius of Boundary, who will try to reach herb and remain where it is. Dogs sniffing this herb lose their ability to bark. They regain the ability to do so at the next sunrise or sunset.

Melissophillum (bastard balm)

This herb draws to it such beasts that serve man, such as bees, and cattle, and horses. If it is bound to the body of such a beast, even if it is wild, it becomes tame and follows the one who bound the herb to it wherever he goes.

Uncommon
Wild Vis: 2
Standard Vis: 1 (Rego)
If this herb is placed on the body of an animal, the animal acts as if it is under the influence of the spell The Gentle Beast (ReAn 20) for as long as the herb is there. This power only works on domesticated species of animals.

Nepeta (pennyroyal)

This herb grows close to the ground and small-leafed, and has a strong smell. Any person or beast who eats of it will be made sterile for a season. If the smell is put close into the nostrils of any person or beast or vermin, it will fall down as if dead, but rise up again after a little while.

Common
Wild Vis: 1
Standard Vis: 0
Anyone who deeply inhales the scent of Nepeta immediately collapses and seems dead for a few minutes. After that he wakes up, unharmed by the experience.

Papaver (poppy)

This herb puts forth a flower as soft as silk and as red as blood. It grows only in places where someone has died. The flower gives milk, and anyone drinking of it will not suffer, nor feel pain or fear.

This same flower, when burned in a lamp, will make visible all airy spirits and bring forth spirits of the dead, so that anyone who sits beside the burning lamp may hear them clearly, and speak and walk with them in their places as with mortal men and women on the earth. This has been proved by experiment in our own time.

Common
Wild Vis: 2
Standard Vis: 1 (Mentem)
Any who drinks the sap of the Papaver suffers no penalties from wounds, and is immune to fear for the next full day.
Burning a papaver acts just like casting the spell Vision of the Haunting Spirit (MuMe 5). All spirits within 15 paces become visible and audible until they leave the vicinity of the lamp.

Pentaphyllon (cinquefoil)

This herb grows low and spreading, with a little flower and a leaf like a man's hand. Its virtue gives eloquence to anyone who bears it, and the power to persuade others to give work and favors to the bearer. This virtue may touch the most powerful, even kings and magi.

Common
Wild Vis: 1
Standard Vis: 0

Anyone who carries this herb receives +3 to rolls using Charm and Leadership.

Semperviva (houseleek)

This herb grows in rocks and upon the roofs of houses, and has a form like the organ of generation. It does not die, even in the most bitter weather and in the most wasted places. Any person or beast who eats of this herb will be cured of poison, and may survive on bad food and water, or little, or none, for as long as the Semperviva is tasted each day. If food and water is good and abundant, any person or beast who eats of this herb will be filled with passion, and be most fertile.

Common
Wild Vis: 1
Standard Vis: 0
This herb, if ingested daily, cures all damage caused by poison. Furthermore, the eater does not require food and water that day. If eaten with adequate food and water, the herb gives +1 to all the eater's personality traits and adds a new trait, Lustful +3, for the day. Eating this herb guarantees offspring from any unions during that day.
One measure of semperviva provides enough material for a full week of consumption.

Serpentina (checkerlily)

This herb grows low to the ground, and bears a flower like a serpent's head. If it is put in any place, red and green serpents will come from that place in great numbers. If the powder of this herb is put into a lamp, all within sight of the lamp will see serpents about them.

Uncommon
Wild Vis: 1
Standard Vis: 0
While growing, this herb attracts all serpents within several hundred paces. If the smoke of burning Serpentina is inhaled, all those who breathe the smoke see the illusion of crawling serpents all around them.

Valeriana (valerian)

This herb will put an end to war, strife, hatred, and fighting between people, if it is put into their food or drink when they are gathered together.

Common
Wild Vis: 1
Standard Vis: 0
Any who ingest this herb act as if under the influence of the spell Calm the Motion of the Heart (PeMe 15). Anger, hatred, jealousy are all calmed by eating this herb.

Verbena (vervain)

This herb has such a virtue that no one who carries it may be touched by infernal things, or harmed by airy spirits. If it is given to one who is possessed by spirits, the spirits will be cast out.

An airy spirit will come to any person who carries it, and come to any place where it is planted. These spirits delight in the teaching of children, and the advising of men and women, and the making of places profitable and well-kept. Though they cannot touch one who carries the herb, they may speak and be heard by the bearer of the herb at all times, and perchance by others. Such spirits are strong-natured, and have been known to be jealous of lovers, or to hate rivals, of the bearer of the herb.

Common
Wild Vis: 1
Standard Vis: 0
Any person who carries this herb attracts the attention of a friendly airy spirit. This ghost (whose Might is 20) advises the bearer and attempts to protect him from all hostile spirits or demons. If planted in the ground, that place is guarded by such a spirit.

Beasts of Virtue

Beasts of virtue have diverse forms, some familiar to any villein, others wonderful and strange. All have forms of flesh, as other beasts do, but their nature is different even among those that resemble beasts of the ordinary kind. It is clear, for instance, that the Hircus whose blood is hot enough to soften Adamas is not the same as a common cotter's goat. Many scholars have also noted great differences among various reports of dragons and other such creatures.

A short list of beasts of virtue follows, which any observant and well-traveled scholar may add to.

Statistics for each type of beast follow their descriptions. Their statistics follow the format found in the Bestiary chapter of ArM4.

Note that all beast attacks occur at Touch range.

Aquila (eagle)

This beast bears the form of an eagle. It is found only where the sun is brightest. It may fly up to the sun and burn any sickness or age from its feathers, and any film from its eyes, so that it has the longest life and keenest sight of any creature. It bears the fire of the sun upon its feathers, so that anyone who carries one will never feel cold or see darkness, for as long as it is carried.

Anyone who looks long upon the beast flying and does not look away will have all film burned from the eyes, and will forever after have the greatest keenness of sight.

> *Rare*
> *Wild Vis: 24*
> *Standard Vis: 12 (Ignem)*
> *Those who carry the feathers of an Aquila are immune to cold. Also, the feathers give off light equal to that of a lantern. The feathers of an Aquila, collectively, are worth 12 pawns of Ignem vis.*
> *Seeing an Aquila in flight permanently grants the viewer the +1 Virtue Keen Vision. However, because of its brightness, a Stamina roll of 9+ is required to remain fixed on an aquila in flight.*

Camelus (camel)

This beast is found in the Holy Land, and has a crooked back. Its blood, put upon the face of anyone, will bring visions. If the blood is put into

Aquila

Characteristics: Cun +2, Per +3 (+6 for vision), Pre +4, Str +1, Sta +5, Dex +3, Qik +3

Magic Might: 20

Size: –1

Personality Traits: Regal +5, Merciful +3

Attack	Init	Atk	Dfn	Dam
Claws	+10	+10	+15	+6

Soak: +6

Body Levels: OK, –1, –3, –5, Incapacitated

Powers:

Immune to Heat and Cold, ReIg 15, 0 points: An aquila cannot be harmed by extremes of heat or cold.

Camelus

Characteristics: Cun –2, Per 0, Pre 0, Str +1, Sta +5, Dex +3, Qik +1

Magic Might: 15

Size: +2

Personality Traits: Lustful +7, Humble +3

Attack	Init	Atk	Dfn	Dam
Bite	+5	+5	+2	+6

Soak: +7

Body Levels: OK, 0/0, –1/–1, –3, –5, Incapacitated

Powers:

Find Water, InAq 15, 5 points: A Camelus can find any surface water within one day's journey of its present location.

Immune to Heat, ReIg 10, 0 points: A Camelus cannot be harmed by extreme heat, even after lengthy exposure.

---

a lamp, and all other lights are put out, spirits may be seen, both airy spirits and also the spirit that dwells in every person, seen as if worn upon their faces.

> *Very Rare*
> *Wild Vis: 10*
> *Standard Vis: 0*
> *Putting the blood of a Camelus on your face will cause a vision relating to a desired subject. Burning the blood of a camelus acts just like the spell Vision of the Haunting Spirit (MuMe 5). All spirits within 15 paces become visible and audible until they leave the vicinity of the lamp.*

Hircus (buck goat)

This beast lives as a goat buck. He is conceived through the ear of his mother, and born through the mouth. There is no height he cannot climb. His blood has such virtue that nothing can withstand it. Any thing which is boiled in his blood, even the hardest stone, is rendered soft, and may be set into any shape.

> *Common*
> *Wild Vis: 20*
> *Standard Vis: 10 (Muto)*
> *The boiled blood affects anything warmed within with an effect like Rock of Viscid Clay (MuTe 15). The blood of a Hircus is worth 10 pawns of Muto vis.*

Leo (lion)

This beast is the ruler of all beasts, by nature of its virtue. No beast will attack it, and all must obey, excepting the Serpens. Those who are with it, or who are girded with its skin, will fear nothing. Other beasts flee from anyone who carries a part of its body, and obey anyone who is with this beast.

> *Very Rare*
> *Wild Vis: 6*
> *Standard Vis: 3 (Rego)*
> *Those who carry or wear the entire skin of a Leo are immune to all fear. Also, all natural animals flee from the carrier. The mane of a leo is worth 3 pawns of Rego vis*

Tasso (badger)

This beast lives in the earth, and grows great claws. It is an invincible fighter, and without fear. Anyone who travels with this beast, or carries its claws, will cause fear in all enemies and kindness in all friends.

> *Common*
> *Wild Vis: 6*
> *Standard Vis: 0*
> *Any who carries the claws of a Tasso receives +2 to his Leadership score when dealing with enemies and +1 to his Charm score when dealing with others.*

Serpens (serpent)

This beast of virtue is well-known, and moves freely in all places, whether earth or water, or under the earth, or in places where airy spirits dwell. It is neither male nor female, young nor old, for it may change itself as it wills by the changing of its skin, becoming new always. This beast knows all things on the earth or under it, as well as in other places, and can teach the language of all animals, the cures for all sicknesses, or whatever else it chooses. Any person eating of it will become changeable as the beast itself.

Hircus

Characteristics: Cun +1, Per +4, Pre +3, Str +1, Sta +1, Dex 0, Qik +1

Magic Might: 10

Size: −1

Personality Traits: Daring +3

Attack	Init	Atk	Dfn	Dam
Horns	+5	+7	+5	+6

Soak: +6

Body Levels: OK, −1, −3, −5, Incapacitated

Powers:

Climb, ReAn 25, 0 points: A Hircus can climb any surface to any height, without fail.

Leo

Characteristics: Int +2, Per +4, Pre +6, Com +2, Str +5, Sta +5, Dex +2, Qik +2

Magic Might: 30

Size: +2

Personality Traits: Regal +5, Proud +3

Attack	Init	Atk	Dfn	Dam
Bite	+15	+15	+12	+23

Soak: +14

Body Levels: OK, 0/0 −1/−1, −3, −5, Incapacitated

Powers:

Roar, CrMe 25, 3 points: When a Leo roars, all who hear it must make a Brave Personality Trait roll of 9+ or freeze in terror.

Command, ReAn 25, 1 point: A Leo can command any other animal except a serpens.

Tasso

Characteristics: Cun +2, Per +4, Pre 0, Str 0, Sta +6, Dex +2, Qik –1

Magic Might: 15

Size: –2

Personality Traits: Fearless +4, Cautious +1

Attack	Init	Atk	Dfn	Dam
Claws	+4	+7	+5	+11

Soak: +10

Body Levels: OK, –1, –5, Incapacitated

Powers:

Inspire Fear, CrMe 15, 1 point: A Tasso may inspire fear in an enemy, who must make a Brave Personality Trait roll of 9+ or flee the Tasso.

Inspire Kindness, CrMe 15, 0 points: A Tasso may inspire kindness in its friends or those who are well-disposed to it.

Serpens

Characteristics: Int +4, Per +2, Pre 0, Com +1, Str –2, Sta +2, Dex +2, Qik +4

Magic Might: 40

Size: –2

Personality Traits: Wise +4, Mutable +3

Attack	Init	Atk	Dfn	Dam
Bite	+12	+10	+10	+2

Soak: +3

Body Levels: OK, –1, –5, Incapacitated

Abilities: Chirurgy 5, Herbalism 5, Medicine 5

Any person who finds a serpens eating an herb and eats of this same herb, will become young always and never grow old.

Common
Wild Vis: 2
Standard Vis: 1 (Muto)

Anyone eating the flesh of a Serpens may change his appearance (but must remain human). It is possible to look like a specific individual if the person has been clearly seen, or to create any desired appearance. Eating the flesh of a single Serpens only allows a single change. This change is permanent, and may only be changed again by magic or though eating the flesh of another Serpens. Presence and Communication cannot be raised by more than 2 each though eating the flesh of a Serpens, since both depend as much on character as appearance and voice. The flesh of a Serpens is worth 1 pawn of Muto vis.

Tasting a herb eaten by a Serpens removes all Decrepitude and afflictions gained through aging from the character who eats it. In addition, this character now has eternal youth, and never again needs to make aging rolls or fear death from old age.

The herb will only work for the one person who actually saw the Serpens taste the herb of its own free will. If this herb is given to another it has no effect. Coercing or bargaining with a Serpens to taste of a plant negates the magical effect. Locating and following a Serpens is possible, but it is likely that one might follow a Serpens for decades before actually seeing it partake of an herb.

A Serpens knows the languages of all creatures.

Guardian Spirits

Each guardian spirit attaches itself to a man or woman, and may not be separated from him without some great crisis. Some say that every mortal born has such a guardian spirit, but their talk seems to refer to the spirits called shadows below. Guardian spirits seem to be found only in the company of certain people. Hermetic magi are heard to say that these spirits are connected to what they term "the Gift," while Cathars will tell that only their perfected ones have such a spirit, churchmen preach of the action of the Holy Spirit in the saints, those of simple faith speak of guardian angels, and so on, each according to his own habits.

Shadows

These spirits are found in the company of every man and woman born, yet much mystery attaches to their nature and their purpose. The theory best argued teaches that the shadow is the visible evidence of a person's own spirit (though not of his soul, which cannot be seen by mortal eyes). What truth may be gleaned suggests that these spirits may appear in the form of the person connected to them, though their usual shape is of the person's shadow.

Those who have had their natures altered, either by magi, or other spirits, or infernal pacts, change the bonds that hold the spirit, so that it may appear as a different shadow than expected from the body, or may even wander abroad. Pagans speak of sending forth their shadows using foreign magics, or in dreams. It is known that certain hedge wizards have the power to send their shadows forth, and to steal shadows.

Whatever such a spirit knows or discovers it may give to its mortal. Some mortals are knowledgeable concerning shadows, as were the ancients who wrote of the genius of a man and the juno of a woman whispering into the ear. Such people may hear their shadow's words as if spoken by a living person. Others may be informed in curious dreams. Some mortals, when such spirits aid them, merely say that luck is with them, ignorant utterly of the means by which they avoid difficulty, or know what they know.

It has been reported that these spirits are released by the death of the mortal body, but that harm rendered to the spirit damages the man or woman in some inward way, without visible wound. It would perhaps be useful to consider ghosts as the shadows of people no longer living. It is certain that the ghosts of pagans and those who have no Christian burial are easiest for the wizard to bring forth, and that the shadows of diabolists are much distorted to the eyes of careful observers. If shadow, spirit, and ghost are words describing the same nature in various guises, much would be made sensible to the observer concerning these things.

Spirit masters are able to summon shadows, both those that are attached to the living and those that are unattached, according to the standard rules for summoning. A shadow that is attached to a person when it is summoned may either detach itself or compel its owner to be summoned as well, depending on the circumstances and the nature of the owner.

A spirit master is the only type of hedge wizard that is able to detach its shadow from its body at will, and then only when the shadow is the spirit master's ally. See "Allies" on page @@ for more information.

Hermetic magi could conceivably use magic to separate their bodies from their shadows. Rego Mentem would be used, with an Imáginem requisite, for such a feat. The basic level for detachment would be 30.

Elemental Spirits

These spirits are made manifest from some worldly element that they are related to, and may appear in solid form. They are of six types, those of fire, air, water, earth, regions beneath the earth, and the lucifugum, who are of darkness and things unseen.

These spirits are not the manifestations of the elements themselves—those are the true elementals, which will be given their own treatment in a future **Ars Magica** supplement.

Salamandrus

This spirit appears as a small lizard. It may sometimes be seen coming out of fires, and cannot be summoned without a newly-stoked fire nearby. It cannot be burned by any fire, and nothing that it touches can be burned. The slime of its body condenses into the stone Asbestos on contact with the air. Its skin is formed of the same stone. The salamandrus may see into places where fires are burning, and speak of what has happened there.

The skin of a Salamandrus is worth 4 pawns of Ignem vis.

Salamandrus

Characteristics: Int –2, Per +2, Pre 0, Com 0, Str –3, Sta +5, Dex +5, Qik +5

Magic Might: 20

Size: –4

Personality Traits: Impetuous +3, Timid +3

Attack	Init	Atk	Dfn	Dam
Claws	0	–6	–6	–12

Soak: +15

Body Levels: OK, –1, –5, Incapacitated

Powers:

Knowledge of Fire, InIg 30, 5 points: A Salamandrus can see as if it were looking out of any fire.

Create Asbestos, CrIg 30, 15 points: A Salamandrus can create one pawn of Asbestos by using this power.

Immune to Fire and Ignem, PeIg 30: A Salamandrus cannot be harmed by fire or Ignem effects.

Halcyon

Characteristics: Int +2 , Per +3, Pre +3, Com +2, Str –3, Sta 0, Dex +3, Qik +5

Magic Might: 10-30

Size: –3

Personality Traits: Alert +5, Curious +3

Attack	Init	Atk	Dfn	Dam
Beak	0	–4	+18	–4

Soak: +5

Body Levels: OK –1, –5 Incapacitated

Powers:

Master of Winds, (level) points: A Halcyon can create any Auram effect of a level less than or equal to its Might.

Halcyon

This spirit appears as a shining bird, blue and white and red, with a wild face. It may only be summoned out of doors, with the wind blowing. It may fly without ceasing, and stir up or calm the winds by the beating of its wings, so much as even to lift a man like a leaf into the air. In this way it calms the waters of the sea and nests on them in the summertime, for its nature is such that it may never touch the earth. It has the power to bring sweet air into any place, such as beneath the water or into a room whose air is foul. It may hear all words spoken out of doors.

A Halcyon's feathers are worth 4 pawns of Auram vis. A single Halcyon feather produces the constant effect of Chamber of Spring Breezes (CrAu 5)

Siren

This spirit has a woman's face and body, but the parts below are winged. It may only be sum-

moned from the water. It dives down into the water, and rises up to sing. It sings so sweetly that all who hear it are charmed and may do nothing but listen to the song, trying to come closer to it for as long as it lasts. Many suppose Sirens to be beautiful, like the women of the water faeries, because of their voices. This is not the case.

The Siren may stir up and bring down the water in an alchemist's vessel or in a bay or port, in fresh water or salt. It has knowledge of all words spoken and things which have taken place upon ships at sea.

A Siren's tongue is worth 4 pawns of Mentem vis. Carrying the tongue of a Siren confers the Exceptional Ability Enchanting Music at a score of 2 for as long as it is carried.

Basilisk

This spirit is the king of serpents, and appears as a great serpent with a crown upon its head. It may only be summoned upon dry land. The Basilisk has a wide throat and a great voice, and may call forth other serpents and such creatures as crawl on the surface of the earth. It has a great poison with which it can strike the eyes of its enemies if it wishes, so that they are blinded after looking at it. It has knowledge of all things which have happened upon the surface of the ground, in contact with the earth.

The crown of a Basilisk is worth 4 pawns of Terram vis.

Siren

Characteristics: Int 0, Per 0, Pre +3, Com +6, Str +2, Sta +3, Dex +2, Qik +2

Magic Might: 10-40

Size: 0

Personality Traits: Seductive +5, Mutable +3

Attack	Init	Atk	Dfn	Dam
<none>	—	—	+5*	—

*+12 in open water

Soak: +5 (+15 in open water)

Body Levels: OK, –1, –3, –5, Incapacitated

Powers:

Enchanting Voice, ReMe 35, 3 points: When Sirens sing, all who hear them must travel towards the sound as long as they are able.

Knowledge of Water, (level) points: A Siren can create any Intéllego, Perdo or Rego Aquam effect of a level less than or equal to its Might.

Breathe Water, 0 points: A Siren may breathe water and not drown.

Basilisk

Characteristics: Int +2, Per +4, Pre +3, Com +3, Str +1, Sta +5, Dex +3, Qik +5

Magic Might: 20-40

Size: –1

Personality Traits: Regal +5, Proud +3

Attack	Init	Atk	Dfn	Dam
Bite	+12	+10	+12	+8*

*Plus poison. The victim must make a Stamina stress roll of 12+ or three Body levels are lost. Otherwise, one Body level is lost (in addition to any lost outright from the attack).

Soak: +10

Body Levels: OK, –1, –3, –5, Incapacitated

Powers:

Controlling Serpents, ReAn 35, 1 point: A Basilisk may call and control all serpents within a mile.

Blind, PeCo 20, 3 points: A Basilisk may strike any creature or person blind upon making eye contact.

Knowledge of Earth, (level) points: A Basilisk may create any Intéllego Terram effect of a level less than or equal to its Might.

Knowledge of the Crawling Creatures, InTe 40, 10 points: A Basilisk can know details of any event which has happened in direct contact with earth or stone.

Amphisbaena

This spirit appears as a very great worm, soft and pale. It has its head equally at either end, and sees without eyes. It can only be summoned beneath the ground, or in a place where the ground has been turned up. Though it seems soft in its body, it may move quickly through any place which is beneath the earth, even if it is of very solid rock. Sometimes it leaves a trail behind it through the stone that mortals can follow. It has a spine in its tail by which it strikes people who have offended it. It seems that this spine has no poison, yet those who are struck often die in falls of rock at some later time. It has a voice like a man, and often speaks without letting itself be seen. It is easily offended. The Amphisbaena knows where all things are which have been put into the ground, and may see into any place beneath the ground and hear what happens there.

4 pawns of Terram vis can be found in the tail-spine of an Amphisbaena. Holding the tail-spine allows the bearer to move through earth.

Amphisbaena

Characteristics: Int 0, Per +1, Pre –3, Com 0, Str 0, Sta +2, Dex –1, Qik +1

Magic Might: 25

Size: 0

Personality Traits: Touchy +3, Knowledgeable +3

Attack	Init	Atk	Dfn	Dam
Tail Sting Curse*	+7	+8	+5	+5,

*Anyone stung by a Amphisbaena (that is, anyone who would have sustained a Body level worth of damage otherwise) will be in a dangerous rock fall or otherwise suffer damage from stone within the next season. This damage may or may not be fatal.

Soak: +15

Body Levels: OK, –1, –3, –5, Incapacitated

Powers:

Pass the Earth, 0 points. An Amphisbaena may pass through any earth or stone.

Create Passage, 1 point per 10 paces: Creates a passage through the earth the Amphisbaena passes through.

Knowledge of the Subterranean, InTe 40, 3 points: See or hear anything occurring under the earth, or know the location of anything buried in the earth.

Lucifugus

Characteristics: Int +5, Per +5, Pre ?, Com –2, Str 0, Sta +3, Dex +5, Qik +5

Magic Might: 30

Size: –2

Personality Traits: Secretive +5, Cold +4

Attack	Init	Atk	Dfn	Dam
Touch	+15	+10	+10*	Cold**

*+20 in darkness

**Upon sustaining damage, the target must make a stress roll + Stamina of 9+ or die. If the rolls succeeds the target loses 3 Body levels in addition to any damage done otherwise.

Soak: +15

Body Levels: OK, –3, –5, Incapacitated

Powers:

Create Darkness, PeIg 15, 2 points: The sphere of darkness so created is 10 paces is diameter, and lasts as long as the Lucifugus remains within it.

Know Secret, 10 points: A Lucifugus can know any secret.

Secretive: No magic can make a Lucifugus reveal its secrets.

Lucifugus

This spirit is called by some the shunsun, or flee-the-light, and no mortal has seen its form. It may only be summoned in utter darkness. Some say it resembles a spider, and is found most often where silver is brought from the earth.

The Lucifugus has no love for men and women, for they kindle many lights and are always looking at things. Its nature is such that any mortal thing touched by it dies, for it is very cold.

It knows secrets, and all things such as no mortal has ever seen, but nothing which is common or transpires in the light. It is said not to like to tell secrets, and will not tell anything if there are many who would learn it. Sometimes it will tell one thing which is hidden in exchange for the hiding of another thing which is known. The Lucifugus whispers, and is difficult to understand.

Spirits of Sickness

These spirits are said by some to be under the rule of infernal powers, but this theory owes more to their nature, which is malignant towards us, than to any experience. It is certain that the causes of sickness are hard to understand, sometimes coming from the bad air of swamps and slaughterhouses, other times from demonic possession, or spirits, or the action of the moon. Since it is observed that wild creatures sometimes suffer sickness, where infernal powers can have no interest, and sickness can be visited upon human beings or livestock by powers which are not infernal, learned scholars define a category of spirits concerned with the causing of sickness. These spirits can be visited upon a person or a beast by those with the power to bend them to their will. This power may be of infernal origin, or divine, as in the Book of Job, or faerie, or of any other type.

Spirits of sickness come in diverse shapes and kinds, just as sickness does. It is said that they often appear to those who can see them as creatures compounded of the parts of different vermin, such as scorpions, worms, rats, mad dogs, or as human creatures bearing heavily the particular marks of the sicknesses they bring. Each kind has the power to enter a person to bring about one kind of sickness and no other, and it must enter into the person to do so. When the spirit leaves the body of the sufferer, the victim is cured, just as is seen in demonic possessions. The death of a sufferer releases the spirit to infect others.

When a disease spirit tries to enter a person, it makes a stress roll + Might against an ease factor of 9 + the victim's Stamina. The ease factor is further modified by +3 if the victim has the Virtue Rapid Convalescence, by the victim's Corpus score if he has one, and by the victim's score in the Exceptional Ability Healer if he has it. The target's state of health is also used as a modifier; fatigue and wound penalties are subtracted from the ease factor. Success for the spirit means infection is successful. Failure means that the victim stays healthy, and the spirit spends five points of Might.

The conditions for recovery below assume that no other action is taken to cure the affliction. Magical spells or other methods of banishing these spirits can be used as well. Disease spirits can be seen with the spells Vision of the Haunting Spirit (MuMe 5), Physician's Eye (InCo 5) and Revealed Flaws of the Mortal Flesh (InCo 10), or with a Second Sight + Perception stress roll of 12+.

Gentle Touch of the Purified Body (CrCo 15) can be used to drive off spirits of sickness. The penetration total must exceed the spirit's Might. Restoration of the Defiled Body (CrCo 25) also drives off spirits of disease if the penetration exceeds the spirit's Might, but it also heals any damage that the spirit caused.

Sample spirits of sickness are listed on page 78 with appropriate Might scores. These certainly don't represent all the spirits of sickness in Mythic Europe.

Warts

Might: 6

Effect: A large wart grows somewhere on the victim.

Recovery: The wart must be physically removed. Then, a stress die + Stamina roll of 9+ is required, or the wart returns.

Fever

Might: 12

Effects: The victim is feverish, is always Weary (–1), and must roll a stress die + Stamina of 6+ each week or become worse. Fever victims who fail their rolls gain one more "permanent" level of fatigue.

Recovery: Fever victims must roll each week to recover, after rolling to see if they become worse. A stress die + Stamina roll of 9+ is required to recover.

Pneumonia

Might: 15

Effects: The victim develops a cough, experiencing alternating fever and chills. The victim is Tired (–3) until cured.

Recovery: Recovering from Pneumonia requires a Stamina stress roll of 12+. Rolls may be made once a week until the victim either dies by failing to roll at least a 6+ or recovers.

Tuberculosis

Might: 15

Effects: The victim becomes short of breath and loses one Fatigue level immediately. One additional Fatigue level is lost each month unless the victim recovers. After all Fatigue levels are lost, Body levels are lost until the victim dies.

Recovery: Bed rest and attention from a skilled healer are required for recovery. Every month of attention allows a recovery roll: a Stamina stress roll of 12+ is required. The victim can gain a +3 to recovery rolls if he moves to a hot, dry climate.

Leprosy

Might: 18

Effects: A full year passes before the first symptoms appear. Initially, a skin rash appears in the extremities, and worsens to include loss of feeling and general weakness. The victim loses one point of Quickness and Presence per year affected. Additionally, one point of Stamina, Strength, or Dexterity (storyguide's choice) is lost per year. Furthermore, unless the victim takes extreme care, he may lose fingers, toes, or other extremities by accident or gangrene.

Lepers are also socially disadvantaged—no one wants them around. They may be forced out of cities or forced to live in leper colonies.

Recovery: There is no recovery without magic or other outside intervention. Even if the victim recovers, reduced Characteristics are not regained.

Pox

Might: 25

Effects: Two weeks after infection, the victim is beset by chills, headache, and fever. A few days later, these symptoms disappear and the pox appears, covering the victim's body with lesions. During this time, the victim operates at a –5 to his Communication and Presence.

Recovery: If not treated in some other way, the victim may make a single recovery roll one week after the appearance of the pox; a Stamina stress roll of 9+ is required. If it fails, the victim will eventually die. If it succeeds, the victim recovers, though he gains the Flaw Disfigured (ArM4, page 47).

Black Death

Might: 30

Effects: A few days after infection, the victim develops painful swellings on his neck and underarms. This is followed by a high fever, leading to delirium, shock, coma, and death. Reduce all characteristics by one each day until the victim dies—typically a few hours to a few weeks.

Recovery: If the victim has the attention of a healer, a single stress roll is allowed. If the host's Stamina + stress die is 12+, he recovers. Lost Characteristics eventually recover to within one point of their original values.

Spirits of Artifice

These spirits dwell in places and objects which are made by artifice, especially if the artifice was produced with the aid of magic. They are found within old buildings, within the towns and cities of the ancients, inside old wells, in the covenants of magi, and in similar places. They may also be found within certain objects, like the statues of great sculptors or the charms of Gifted children. Within auras of magic they may be quite common, attaching themselves to every tool, toy, and pasture wall.

Some say that no sacrifice goes unreceived, so that a spirit is attracted when offerings are made that are not part of divine or infernal ceremonies, or that are not suited to the faeries. In has been shown in our own time that certain children and fools, in making simple offerings out of great need, have brought spirits to them.

The nature of a spirit of artifice is likely to be influenced by the nature of their place, and of the actions which first brought them to mortal eyes.

A spirit of artifice appears in a form resembling its habitation in some way. Though these spirits may be confused with faeries, it is to be remembered that faeries are wary of mortal artifice. They usually respond with fear or fascination to the kinds of places and objects these spirits inhabit.

Most of these spirits are more limited than faeries, divine agents, or infernal powers. They tend to concern themselves only with what would concern the place or object that hosts them. In direct experience, the spirit dwelling in a child's wooden toy horse was much interested in knight-

ly stories, the preservation of wood, and the safety of the child, but not in much else. The spirit of an ancient manor house in Italy has been reported to speak as the house itself, to have a minute knowledge of the affairs of the estate, but to be entirely ignorant of anything beyond its borders. A spirit dwelling in a bust of Aristotle, however, was said to have a full and inquiring nature, and very knowledgeable, as if the spirit wished to live up as well as possible to the form to which it pretended. This last spirit was known to appear to some as if it was the living Aristotle. Such a spirit might be confused with a ghost, or even with a living man.

Spirits of Artifice are not found in every ale mug, chamber pot, and weapon in Mythic Europe. Rather, they are found in items and buildings that are crafted with extra care, crafted within a magical aura, crafted of special material, crafted with strong emotion, or with a combination of the above.

Spirits of Artifice are usually passive, simply existing, and interacting only with those who go out of their way to talk to them. They only become active when their vessels are threatened, or they have a vested interest in something that is going on around them. When that happens, they may be able to animate their vessels, depending on their Might and inclination.

A Spirit of Artifice has a Magical Might based on how old and well-crafted its dwelling is. The Spirit of the Parthenon might have a Might of up to 30; the spirit of a beautiful, but recently made statue would have a Might of 20; the spirit of a modest house would have, at most, a Might of 10. The Might of the child's horse used in the example above would have a Might of 5.